AF608182

THE CATHOLIC UNIVERSITY OF AMERICA
CANON LAW STUDIES
Number 96

CANONICAL CAUSES FOR MATRIMONIAL DISPENSATIONS

AN HISTORICAL SYNOPSIS AND COMMENTARY

A DISSERTATION

Submitted to the Faculty of Canon Law of the Catholic University of America in partial Fulfillment of the Requirements for the Degree of

DOCTOR OF CANON LAW

BY THE

REVEREND WILLIAM A. O'MARA, A.B., J.C.L.,
Priest of the Diocese of Scranton

THE CATHOLIC UNIVERSITY OF AMERICA
WASHINGTON, D. C.
1935

Nihil Obstat;

VALENTINUS T. SCHAAF, O.F.M., J.C.D.,
Censor Deputatus.

Washingtonii, D. C., die XXV mensis Maii, 1935.

Imprimatur;

THOMAS C. O'REILLY, D.D.,
Episcopus Scrantoniensis.

Scrantonii, die XXVII mensis Maii, 1935.

Printed by
THE PAULIST PRESS
New York, N. Y.

TO MY MOTHER

TABLE OF CONTENTS

PART II

HISTORICAL SYNOPSIS

PART III

CANONICAL COMMENTARY

CHAPTER VI

CHAPTER VII

PAGE

CHAPTER VIII

FOREWORD

THE theory of dispensation is founded on the fact that at times circumstances may arise which may make the observance of a common law an undue burden. In such circumstances reason demands that the common law be suspended in order that grave inconvenience and harm be prevented. But in the application of dispensation as in the application of law itself, right reason and the good of the community must be considered and this implies a just cause. No better idea of cause in relation to dispensation can be found than in the words of St. Bernard: "Dispensatio sine justa causa, non dispensatio sed dissipatio est dicenda." [1]

In this dissertation a necessarily brief historical synopsis has been attempted wherein is traced the juridical origin of the canonical cause and the insistence that has always been placed on the cause in dispensatory acts. The historical background of several particular canonical causes has been outlined in an effort to indicate that the causes admitted in modern curial practice are by no means new.

In the canonical commentary more particular emphasis has been placed on those causes for matrimonial dispensations enumerated by the Sacred Congregation for the Propagation of the Faith in an Instruction issued on May 9, 1877. A study has been made of these causes in their canonical aspects and an appraisal of their practical value, especially in curial practice in America, has been attempted.

The writer wishes to express his sincere gratitude to the Most Reverend Thomas C. O'Reilly, D.D., Bishop of Scranton, through whose kindly interest he was permitted to pursue a course in graduate Canon Law studies at the Catholic University of America. In like manner appreciation is extended to the members of the Faculty of the School of Canon Law for their kind and helpful direction, to the Reverend Eugene J. Moriarty, J.C.B., for his gracious assistance in preparing the dissertation for the press and to the many others who have aided and encouraged the writer in the preparation of this work.

[1] *Bernardi Opera Omnia, De Consideratione,* L. III, c. 4.

PART I

PRELIMINARY DISCUSSION

CHAPTER 1

THE VARIOUS USES OF THE WORD DISPENSATION

In tracing the history of the doctrine of dispensation it will be found that it was not until the twelfth century that the strict juridic definition of the term came into being. The Decretist Rufinus (a. 1159) was the author of this strict juridic definition.[1] From the thirteenth century when the canonists became more specific[2] the strict meaning of dispensation as intended by Rufinus became more universally accepted.[3]

Article I. Definition and Application

Without considering the various definitions advanced by individual canonists, for all of them expressed the idea in slightly varying words, it will suffice to note that the modern canonical concept of dispensation is the relaxation of a law in a particular case.[4] The final ecclesiastical approbation has been placed on this signification of the term since this definition, through Canon 80, has been incorporated in the Code. Generally speaking, "dispensation" is the word used in signifying the act by which anyone is released from the obligation of a law. This use of the term is too broad since a person can be released from the obligation of a law in various ways, for instance, through privilege, exemption, interpretation and the like. To be exact the word "dispensation" is used in law to signify the removal of a bond of law in some particular case.[5] Moreover, dispensation is not an act of doctrine or prudence but rather an act of voluntary jurisdiction by which the lawful superior through himself or through the power conceded by him to another[6] takes away the

[1] *Cf. Summa Decretorum des Magister Rufinus*, ed. H. Singer, p. 234.

[2] Vermeersch-Creusen, *Epitome Juris Canonici*, I, n. 187.

[3] *Cf.* Michiels, *Normae Generales*, II, p. 452.

[4] *Cf.* Suarez, *Tractatus de Legibus*, L. VI, c. 10.

[5] *Cf.* Suarez, *Tractatus de Legibus*, L. VI, c. 10.

[6] Canon 80.

obligation proper to a determined law in favor of some physical or moral person or persons who otherwise would be bound by the law. This relaxation of the law can take place only in a special case.[7] Here it is understood that the obligation of the law is taken away only in favor of certain persons, things or circumstances while the obligation of the law in itself remains both for the other subjects in the community and for the other cases and circumstances comprehended by the law. The phrase *in casu speciali* can be applied to the persons, things or circumstances in whose favor the relaxation of the law is granted and it can be extended also to the *vinculum legis* that is suspended. Hence in some instances only a single moral obligation of the law will be removed, as in a dispensation from a particular matrimonial impediment for a specific person, while in other instances a multiple obligation can be the object of a dispensation as would be the case of dispensation, for one or many persons, from the law of fast and abstinence.[8]

Here it will be well to consider the scope of dispensation, that is, those laws from which dispensation is not granted or the *leges indispensabiles* and those laws which from their very nature can be called *leges dispensabiles.*

As a general statement it can be said that through dispensation every positive human law can be relaxed.[9] This principle can be founded on the fact that for human government the power of dispensing from law is not only useful but it is also necessary,[10] for human reason is fallible and oftentimes prudence demands the relaxation of a law in a particular instance that thereby common necessity and utility may be safeguarded. Since ecclesiastical law is likewise positive human law it can also be said that every bond accustomed to be imposed through ecclesiastical law can be dispensed from whether this bond is preceptive or prohibitive, or penal or

[7] Before the Code the expression in a particular case was commonly used.

[8] *Cf.* Michiels, *Normae Generales,* II, p. 454.

[9] *Cf.* Suarez, *Tractatus de Legibus,* L. VI, c. 12, n. 5.

[10] ". . . publice expedit legis vinculum quandoque relaxare, ut plenius, evenientibus casibus et necessitatibus, pro communi utilitate satisfiat." Conc. Trid., sess. XXV. *de ref.,* c. 18.

irritative.[11] Human law depends for its existence on the will of the Superior and likewise through the same will the law is either executed or relaxed.[12]

To modify the general statement it must be said that although a dispensation can be applied to all laws constituted by human ecclesiastical authority there are, however, some grave ordinances from which dispensations are rarely or never granted.[13] These are laws which approach nearer to the divine law or are intimately connected with faith and morals or with the salvation of souls or finally they are laws which regard the public utility of the Church.

In modern canonical jurisprudence laws governing certain impediments are regarded as indispensable laws. These laws form a twofold class. In the first instance the Church cannot dispense from these laws because they are directly connected with the divine law either natural or positive. These laws, in no way depending on the human will, govern: 1, the bond arising from a consummated marriage between two Christians; [14] 2, antecedent and perpetual impotency; [15] 3, consanguinity is the first degree of the direct line.[16]

In the second instance the Church is not accustomed to dispense from certain ecclesiastical laws because these laws approach closely to the divine law and, further, in a very marked degree, they regard

[11] *Cf.* Michiels, *Normæ Generales,* II, p. 467.

[12] *Cf.* Gratian, in dict., 16, c. XXV, q. 1: ". . . Sacrosancta Romana ecclesia jus et auctoritatem sacris canonibus impertit, sed non eis alligatur. . . . Licet itaque sibi contra generalia decreta specialia previlegia indulgere, et speciali beneficio concedere quod generali prohibetur decreto."

[13] Many ancient authors, especially among the Decretists and Decretalists, held some certain laws to be indispensable because they believed these laws pertained to the divine natural and positive law rather than to the ecclesiastical law. Among these indispensable laws they especially numbered the laws of the Apostles and the enactments of the first four ecumenical Councils. *Cf.* Brys, *De Dispensatione,* pp. 77-79.

[14] Canon 1118; Gasparri, *De Matrimonio,* n. 1125; Payen, *De Matrimonio,* II, n. 2186.

[15] Canon 1068, §§ 1, 2; Payen, *De Matrimonio,* I, n. 1001.

[16] Gasparri, *De Matrimonio,* n. 712; Payen, *De Matrimonio,* I, n. 1451; *Cf.* S. C. C., Leodien, 14 December, 1793—*Fontes,* n. 3888; S. C. S. Off., inst. (ad Ep. S. Alberti) 9 December, 1874, n. 18, ad 4 et 5—*Fontes,* n. 1036.

the commonweal and, if they were easily dispensable, could cause untold harm. These laws govern: 1, the impediment of affinity in the direct line arising from a consummated marriage; [17] 2, the impediment arising from the sacred order of priesthood, from which no dispensation is given even in danger of death; [18] 3, the impediment of consanguinity in the first degree of the collateral line, for the impediment is probably of the divine natural law.[19]

Article II. Dispensation from Vindictive Punishments

The Code states that a vindictive punishment can be remitted through dispensation.[20] Properly speaking this remission is not a dispensation even in the wide sense of the term. When a punishment is remitted through dispensation the obligation of the penal law is not relaxed. Rather the mere juridical consequence which is attached to the penal law is removed.[21]

Artcle III. Dispensation from Irregularities and Impediments

The word dispensation is used in its proper juridical signification in these canons in the Code which state that impediments and irregularities for orders and impediments to marriage can be removed through dispensation.[22] An irregularity is, in reality, an impediment[23] and an impediment is a barrier which makes the licit reception of orders and the valid contracting of marriage (in the case of a diriment impediment or the licit contracting in the case of an impeding impediment) an impossibility. When it is stated in law that

[17] Canon 1043; *Cf.* also Canons 97 and 1077; Chelodi, *Jus Matrimoniale,* n. 102; Payen, *De Matrimonio,* I, n. 644.

[18] Canon 1043; Payen, *De Matrimonio,* I, n. 644.

[19] Canon 1076, § 3; S. C. C., *Aesina,* 23 November, 1805—*Fontes,* n. 3926; Augustine, *A Commentary on Canon Law,* V, p. 207; Payen, *De Matrimonio,* n. 1451.

[20] Canons 2236, § 1, and 2289.

[21] *Cf.* Michiels, *Normae Generales,* II, p. 453.

[22] *Cf.* Canons 990 and 1040.

[23] *Cf.* Sipos, *Enchiridion Juris Canonici,* p. 448.

an impediment can be dispensed from, the dispensation accomplishes the very purpose for which the doctrine of dispensation was created in canonical jurisprudence, namely, the bond of the law which places the impediment is relaxed in a particular case and the relaxation makes the licit reception of orders or the valid contracting of marriage a possibility for the one in whose favor the dispensation is granted.

Article IV. Dispensation from Vows and Oaths

The proper object of the *relaxatio legis* in a dispensation strictly taken is the legal bond or the very obligation proper to a determined law. In other words that element of a law which gives it its force either preceptive or prohibitive or penal or irritative is by virtue of the dispensation relaxed.

From this it can be seen that the relaxation of an obligation assumed through a vow or an oath is not a dispensation in the strict sense even though the word dispensation appears in the canons treating of the relaxation of vows and oaths.[24] In these instances the bond of the divine law which determines the obligation arising from the vow or oath and demands its fulfillment is not relaxed (for from this law no human power can dispense) but the Church, through the ministerial power conceded to her, takes away the *object* of the obligation and when this is removed the application of the divine law in a particular case ceases.[25]

Article V. Dispensation *Super Rato*.

In a similar manner the Code speaks of the possibility of dissolving a ratified but not consummated marriage through the medium of a dispensation granted by the Holy See.[26] To be exact this is not

[24] Canons 1311 and 1320.

[25] *Cf.* Michiels, *Normae Generales,* II, p. 453. The Church is able authentically to declare and interpret, and this infallibly, the divine law. Therefore the Pope cannot only declare what causes excuse from the divine law but he can also determine the sense and obligation of the law. *Cf.* Noldin, *De Principiis,* n. 100 (1902).

[26] *Cf.* Canon 1119.

the strict legal use of the term dispensation. When a ratified but not consummated marriage has been dissolved the bond of the law in the sense of Canon 80 is not relaxed but through vicarious power committed to him the Pope simply declares that, while the divine law of the indissolubility of marriage remains intact, the bond of this particular marriage has been dissolved or annulled and the law is no longer binding upon the parties who entered the contract.

Status Quaestionis

It will be the purpose in this dissertation to consider the term dispensation in its strict meaning, namely, the authoritative relaxing of a law in favor of a particular person or circumstance while the obligation of the law remains so far as other persons and circumstances are concerned. Further, only dispensations from matrimonial impediments will be treated and these only in so far as the canonical cause for granting them is concerned.

CHAPTER II

THE AUTHOR OF MATRIMONIAL DISPENSATIONS

THE author of matrimonial dispensations is he who, by ordinary or delegated power concedes a matrimonial dispensation and hence grants the relaxation of an impediment in a particular case.[1]

The legislator can dispense simply because he is the author of the law.[2] If the legislator can abrogate a law, which is a more comprehensive act than dispensation, it follows that he can also relax a law.[3]

The successor of the legislator enjoys the same power as the legislator himself.[4] Hence if the legislator has dispensatory powers his successor can also make use of them. By the same token the superior of the legislator can dispense, for if the legislator himself has such powers it must follow that his superior in matters jurisdictional must have more extended powers, else he could not be regarded as a superior.

Power to dispense from a law can come either by reason of one's office or by direct concession of a faculty. If the dispensation is granted in the first way it is a use of ordinary power. If the one dispensing acts by reason of his faculties he is using delegated power.[5] The power of a delegate follows in logical juridic sequence from the rule, "One can do by another that which he can do by himself."[6] But the delegate acts validly only within the scope of the mandate through which he derives his power.[7]

[1] *Cf.* Payen, *De Matrimonio,* I, n. 628.

[2] "Omnis res, per quascumque causas nascitur, per easdem dissolvitur."—c. 1, X, *de regulis juris,* V, 41.

[3] *Cf.* Cicognani, *Commentarium ad Librum I Codicis,* p. 320.

[4] "Is qui in jus succedit alterius, eo jure, quo ille, uti debebit."—Reg. Juris 46 in VI°.

[5] *Cf.* Canon 197, § 1.

[6] Reg. Juris 68, in VI°.

[7] Canon 203, § 1.

Article I. The Roman Pontiff

The Roman Pontiff by proper authority, can dispense validly and licitly in all ecclesiastical laws whether they were constituted by general or particular councils, by another Pope, or by the Apostles.[8] But he cannot change those Apostolic Canons which the Apostles, as Bishops of the early Church obtained from Christ as the author of those laws, for example, the baptism of infants or the indissolubility of a consummated marriage[9]

In regard to matrimonial dispensations, the Pope cannot dispense from the diriment impediments which have been established by the divine law, either natural or positive, and which are absolute and independent of the act of man. Such impediments would be antecedent and perpetual impotency,[10] the bond of a marriage which has been consummated between two baptized persons,[11] and the first degree of consanguinity in the direct line.[12] In like manner the Pope cannot dispense from the impeding impediments which have been placed absolutely by the divine law, namely, mixed religion or disparity of cult when the danger of perversion has not been removed for the Catholic party and the children.[13]

By vicarious power, the Pope can, for a just cause, validly dis-

[8] C. 4, X, *de concessione praebendae et ecclesiae non vacantis,* III, 8.—Suarez, *Tractatus de legibus,* Lib. VI, c. 12.

In actual practice the Pope in person does not concede dispensations. He dispenses for the external forum through the Holy Office, the Congregation for Religious, the Congregation for the discipline of the Sacraments and the Congregation for the Oriental Church. For the internal forum, he dispenses through the Sacred Penitentiary. Moreover, for those things that pertain to matrimonial dispensations, the Congregation for the Propagation of the Faith is the medium through which such dispensations are obtained for the territory subject to this congregation.

[9] Suarez, *Tractatus de Legibus,* Lib. VI, c. 14, n. 2.

[10] Canon 1068, § 1.

[11] Canon 1118.

[12] Canon 1076 § 1. Likewise the impediment of consanguinity in the first degree of the collateral line can probably be considered an indispensable impediment by force of Canon 1076, § 3.

[13] Canon 1060; Payen, *De Matrimonio,* I, n. 632.

pense from the diriment impediment of ligamen, provided the marriage has not been consummated.[14] This impediment is of the divine law but it does not oblige man immediately and independently of the will of man, as does, for example the divine law of honor toward parents or of love of neighbor. Man has no other alternative but to be obliged by such laws. On the contrary, the impediment of ligamen arising from an unconsummated marriage is of the divine law but the one who is bound by the impediment previously took upon himself the obligation of this divine law and hence the fulfillment of this law rests on the human will of man. When the Pope dispenses from this law his act is not a dispensation in the strict sense for a dispensation is the relaxation of a law in a particular case. In the instance of dispensation from an unconsummated marriage, "the Pope, by reason of his vicarious power, directly concedes the favor of solution of the bond of a ratified marriage; consequently, the matter being removed, the divine law on ligamen no longer binds." [15]

While the Pope can dispense from all impediments of the ecclesiastical law, he does not use his power to the fullest extent. In virtue of his high office it is for him to hold in highest regard the laws of the Church and while he himself is above his own laws he would be betraying a sacred trust in indiscriminately dispensing from every ecclesiastical law.[16] Hence, while he is able, he is not accustomed to grant dispensations from the impediments of age,[17] sacred orders, especially from priesthood,[18] abduction,[19] from public conjugicide,[20]

[14] Canon 1119.

[15] Wernz, *Jus Decretalium*, IV, p. 618.

[16] St. Paul says: " . . . according to the power which is given me unto edification and not unto destruction." II Cor. c. 13.

[17] S. C. S. Off., 24 November, 1866—*Collect.*, n. 1382.

[18] Vlaming, *Praelectiones Juris Matrimonii*, I, n. 306b.

[19] Vlaming, *Praelectiones Juris Matrimonii*, I, n. 311—S. C. S. Off., 15 June, 1875.

[20] The Church does not dispense from this impediment either for contracting or revalidating marriage. Bishops are empowered, however, in virtue of Canon 1043 to dispense from this impediment in danger of death.—*Cf.* Vlaming, *Praelectiones Juris Matrimonii*, I, n. 328b.

or from affinity in the direct line, especially when the marriage has been consummated.[21]

Article II. The Ordinary

By Canon 81 of the Code it is forbidden to Ordinaries *Cf.* Canon 198, § 1, under the Roman Pontiff to dispense from the general laws of the Church even in a particular case. But by the same canon the Ordinary is permitted to dispense in general ecclesiastical laws when this power is explicitly or implicitly conceded to him, and when it is a question of a case from which the Holy See is accustomed to dispense and there is difficulty in recourse and grave harm in delay. Matrimonial impediments are general laws of the Church and hence the Ordinary cannot dispense from them unless faculties have been explicitly or implicitly granted to him or unless the other two conditions mentioned in Canon 81 are verified, namely, when there is danger in delay and when the case is one in which the Holy See is accustomed to grant dispensation.

By virtue of his ordinary vicarious power the Ordinary can dispense from doubtful impediments if the doubt is one of fact and concerns an impediment from which the Holy See is accustomed to grant dispensation.[22]

1. *In Danger of Death*

In virtue of Canon 1043 the local Ordinary enjoys a two-fold faculty of dispensing, namely for contracting or convalidating marriage when danger of death is present.[23] He can use his faculties for soothing the conscience of the stricken party or, if needful, for legitimatizing the children. In danger of death he can dispense from the form prescribed to be observed in marriage, *i. e.*, he can dis-

[21] If the marriage from which affinity arises is not consummated, the Church will grant a dispensation even if the relationship is in the first degree. If the marriage is consummated the Church will for a grave cause dispense in cases of lineal affinity beyond the first degree. Wahl, *The Matrimonial Impediments of Consanguinity and Affinity*, p. 90.

[22] Canons 15, 81, 1043.

[23] Wernz-Widal, *Jus Matrimoniale*, V., n. 413.

pense with the presence of either the competent priest or of the witnesses or even from the presence of both.[24] And further he can dispense from all the impediments of the eccclesiastical law either public or occult or even multiple, except those impediments arising from sacred priesthood and from affinity in the direct line if the marriage has been consummated. The dispensation can be granted to the proper subjects of the Ordinary wherever they may be living and likewise to all those living in his territory provided no scandal will arise from such a concession.

2. *In Urgent Cases*

Outside the danger of death and for the same reasons the Ordinary can dispense from all the impediments enumerated in Canon 1043,[25] provided that the case is urgent, namely "if the impediment is discovered when all preparations have been made for the wedding and the marriage cannot be delayed, without probable danger of serious harm, until a dispensation is obtained from the Holy See." [26] By virtue of this canon the Ordinary can also use his faculties in convalidating a marriage if the same danger in delay is present and there is no time for recourse to the Holy See.[27]

3. *In Ordinary Circumstances*

Outside the case of urgency the Ordinary can dispense from the banns of marriage [28] and from vows that are not reserved.[29]

[24] Canon 1094.

[25] The opinion seems to be more probable which holds that Canon 1045 does not grant faculties to dispense from the form of celebration as well as from all ecclesiastical impediments enumerated in Canon 1043. The probability of this opinion is based on the fact that Canon 1045 mentions only impediments and is silent concerning the form of marriage. Furthermore, Canon 1045 is to be applied to those cases which exist outside the danger of death and unless death threatens there will be less occasion to dispense from the form of celebration. *Cf.* Payen, *De Matrimonio,* I, n. 648; Ayrinhac-Lydon, *Marriage Legislation in the New Code of Canon Law,* n. 77.

[26] Canon 1045, § 1.

[27] Canon 1045, § 2.

[28] *Cf.* Canon 1028.

[29] Canon 1313, n. 1.

Article III. The Pastor and the Assisting Priest

1. *In Danger of Death*

When there is danger of death the pastor and the priest who assists at the marriage according to the prescriptions of Canon 1098, n. 2, namely, when he assists at a marriage in the absence of the Ordinary, the pastor or the delegated priest who cannot be present or approached without serious inconvenience, enjoy the same powers as the local Ordinary for all those cases and conditions mentioned in Canon 1043. But they can use these faculties only when it is impossible to approach the local Ordinary.[80] It can be considered that the Ordinary cannot be approached when it is feared that the party will die or lapse into unconsciousness before the response can come from the Ordinary or when, in the instance of an occult case it is feared that there is danger of violating the secret.[81]

The pastor can dispense from the form of celebration and from all the ecclesiastical impediments except the two excluded by Canon 1043, namely, that impediment arising from priestly orders and that from affinity in the direct line arising from a consummated marriage. In like manner the priest assisting at a marriage in virtue of Canon 1098, n. 2, enjoys the same faculties as does the pastor, that is, he can dispense from the form of marriage and from all impediments of the ecclesiastical law except the two excluded by Canon 1043.[82]

2. *In Urgent Cases*

When there is no danger of death the pastor and the assisting priest can dispense from all the impediments mentioned in Canon 1043, § 1, but only when the case is urgent, *viz.*, when everything

[80] Canon 1044.

[81] Extraordinary means of approach need not be used.—*Cf.* Cappello, *De Matrimonio*, III, n. 236, 2a. In a reply of the Code Commission it is stated that in the cases mentioned in Canons 1044, 1045, § 3, it is to be considered that the Ordinary cannot be approached when it is impossible to have recourse to him by letter even though it is possible to reach him by telephone or telegraph.—*Cf.* Reply of Code Commission, 12 November, 1922, V—*A. A. S.*, XIV (1922), p. 662. Moreover it would seem that the use of such modes of communication would oftentimes be the occasion of divulging secrets.

[82] Payen, *De Matrimonio*, I, n. 668—Ayrinhac-Lydon, *Marriage Legislation in the New Code of Canon Law*, n. 75.

is prepared for the wedding and it cannot be postponed, when the Ordinary cannot be approached without danger of violating the seal[33] and only when the case is occult. All three conditions must be present.[34]

Article IV. The Confessor

The confessor possesses the same powers to dispense as the pastor and the assisting priest, both in danger of death and in cases of urgency when there is no danger of death.[35] But his faculties are limited to the internal sacramental forum,[36] and only for occult cases in which the local Ordinary cannot be approached or can be approached only with the danger of violating the seal.[37]

Some authors hold that the confessor in the internal sacramental forum can dispense from impediments which by nature are public but which *in praesenti* are *de facto* occult.[38] Others hold that the confessor by virtue of Canons 1044 and 1045, § 3, can dispense only in those impediments which are occult both by nature and by fact.[39]

The opinion of those limiting the powers of the confessor to the impediments occult both by nature and by fact is intrinsically more probable since it avoids a contradiction between the internal and external forum.[40]

The opinion of those extending the confessor's power to all impediments public by nature but occult by fact can be truly probable for there are cases in which there is scarcely any danger of a conflict between the internal and external forum. In such cases it should be left to the confessor and not to others to dispense from impediments public by nature but occult in fact.[41]

[33] Violating seal—either sacramental or secretum concilii seu officii.

[34] De Smet, *Betrothment and Marriage*, n. 793.

[35] *Cf.* De Smet, *Betrothment and Marriage*, n. 794.

[36] *Cf.* Canon 1044.

[37] *Cf.* Canon 1045, § 3.

[38] Chelodi, *Jus Matri.*, n. 44. Arendt, "Du cas perplexe et des pouvoirs du confesseur d'après le Code"—N. R. Th., 1920, p. 261.

[39] Cappello, *De Matrimonio*, n. 238; Ojetti, *Jus Pont*, 1926, p. 56 ss.; De Smet, *De Sponsalibus*, n. 794; Vermeersch-Creusen, II, n. 312.

[40] *Cf.* Payen, *De Matrimonio*, I, n. 673.

[41] *Cf.* Payen, *De Matrimonio*, n. 673.

PART II

HISTORICAL SYNOPSIS

CHAPTER III

DISPENSATION IN THE EARLY CENTURIES

IN treating the history of dispensation in general most canonists even up to the present time, have arbitrarily terminated the first period of the history with the beginning of the tenth century. This division has been adopted because the history of the first nine centuries is vague. Some claim [1] that no more is known today of dispensations in the first nine centuries than when the canonists first began to write the history of this period.

Before the ninth century no text is found in which the true juridical meaning of the term dispensation is set forth. But many texts can be found among the Fathers where the idea of dispensation is described, although these texts do not have the intention of regarding dispensation in the true juridical sense. These Fathers and early jurists were accustomed to use the terms "indulgence" or "mercy" or "venia." In a wide sense these terms were used to denote any mitigation or favorable change in any ecclesiastical law made for the common good of the Church.[2]

While these early jurists seem to have made no attempt at arriving at the true juridical meaning of the term dispensation nevertheless during these early centuries there are occasional instances of the relaxation of ecclesiastical laws which, when analyzed, conform to the modern canonical conception of the term. Only isolated cases of such true dispensations came down to us although Brys is of the opinion that dispensation occurred in the early centuries with more frequency than is commonly supposed.[3] The greater number of authors, however, hold a negative opinion on this point. Some of these authors [4]

[1] Notably, Freisen, *Geschichte des Canonischen Eherechts*, p. 205.

[2] Michiels, *Normae Generales*, II, p. 450.

[3] Brys, *De Dispensatione in Jure Canonico*, p. 26.

[4] Van Espen, *Jus Eccles. Univ.*, t. II, pars 4, c. 4; Thomassinus, *Vetus et Nova Ecclesiae Disciplina*, t. II, pars 2, L. III, c. 24; De Marca, *De Concordantia Sacerdotii et Imperii*, L. III, c. 13.

hold that, because in the early Church fewer laws existed and were more rigidly observed, fewer dispensations were granted and these only *post factum.*

Article I. Dispensation *Post Factum*

It is certain that in the early centuries a high regard for the sacred canons was held; for Innocent I (402-417) urged that whatever was ordered by the Church should be observed by all;[5] Leo IV (440-461) held that anyone who acted contrary to the canons of the Fathers could not be considered as observing them entirely.[6]

In the first three centuries dispensations from the general laws of the Church and from the Apostolic laws revolved about the matter of irregularities for ordinations and the reconciliation of penitents.[7] This fact implies the existence of dispensations only *post factum* and these are dispensations only in the broad sense. In fact the first instances of dispensation, so called, that can be found are dispensations *post factum.* For example Pope Melchiades (311-314) in the Synod of Rome dispensed from the irregularities incurred by those bishops who had been consecrated at the hands of the Donatists.[8] Later Pope Damasus (368-384) dispensed in the irregularity incurred by Flavian when in the beginning he was doubtfully elected to the See of Antioch.[9]

In the instances quoted the dispensations were granted through papal intercession. Since there are no records of dispensations having been granted earlier than the fourth century and since prior to that time dispensations were granted through episcopal intercession,[10] it is quite probable that such episcopal dispensations were only *post factum.*

Those authors who recognize the existence of dispensation in the

[5] C. 10, D. XI.

[6] C. 16, C. XXVI, q. 1.

[7] *Cf.* Fourneret, *Le Mariage Chretien,* p. 279.

[8] Thomassinus, *Vetus et Nova Ecclesiae Disciplina,* t. II, pars 2, L. III, c. 24, n. 7; Mansi, II, 435.

[9] Thomassinus, o. c., n. 19.

[10] Thomassinus, *Vetus et Nova Ecclesiae Disciplina,* t. II, pars 2, L. III, c. 24, n. 14.

early centuries are agreed that the author of dispensation was the bishop. Some writers [11] declare that the bishops in the first and second and even in the third centuries relaxed the Apostolic canons and decrees when such action was demanded through public necessity. During these centuries they so acted independently of the Roman Pontiff and even of the provincial synod because due to persecutions it was quite impossible to communicate with the Holy See or with other bishops and for the same reason it was impossible to convoke councils. Moreover, in those days the general laws of the Church were few in number for they were for the most part rules contained in the Scriptures and in Apostolic traditions. Since they were held in such high regard in ecclesiastical circles, exceptions from them were infrequent. The positive laws of those days were principally the particular laws enacted by each bishop for his own diocese and these dealt especially with the reconciliation of penitents, with the remission of ecclesiastical punishments and with the irregularities of those who were aspiring to the clerical state.[12]

Article II. Dispensation from the Law

When the period of persecution came to an end the Church grew and became stronger. Naturally her laws became more complex due to the facility with which papal and conciliar legislation could be made for when peace had been restored to the Church it was the natural impulse for the bishops to gather together in councils to make laws governing the faith and discipline of the Church.[13] While dispensations were by no means common during these early centuries a few instances of *ante factum* dispensations can be found. It is true that no matrimonial dispensations, that is, dispensations taken in the strict sense, were given in the early centuries for these came only after the eleventh century,[14] but dispensations from general ecclesi-

[11] Thomassinus, *Vetus et Nova Ecclesiae Disciplina,* t. II, pars 2, L. III, c. 2; Alzog, *Universal Church History,* I, p. 474.

[12] *Cf.* Brys, *De Dispensatione in Jure Canonico,* p. 32.

[13] Alzog, *Universal Church History,* I, p. 474.

[14] Stiegler, *Dispensation, Dispensationswesen und Dispensationsrecht in Kirchenrecht,* p. 278.

astical laws were given as early as the fifth century. In the year 494 Pope Gelasius I gave faculties to the bishops of the Italian peninsula to dispense in the law of interstices because, due to famine and wars, the churches of the region could not adequately be supplied with priests if the laws of interstices was strictly enforced.[15] In another instance Leo I in 446 dispensed a layman that he might be taken directly from the lay state and elevated to the episcopacy notwithstanding the prohibition of this practice as contained in the second canon of the Council of Nicea (325).[16] Finally in 794 Adrian I dispensed from the law of residence that Angilram, Bishop of Metz and Hildebold, Archbishop of Cologne, might reside in the royal palace with Charlemagne.[17] Wernz and Stiegler,[18] regard this historical fact as a true dispensation, while Cicognani and Cocchi hold it as the first instance of a real juridical dispensation.[19]

From these few instances it can be ascertained that dispensations from the law were granted after the fourth century. Moreover it can be seen that the early jurists had a definite idea that for good reasons the sacred canons could at times be relaxed for the common good and utility of the Church. This is clear from the words of Pope Gelasius I: "Aliquando enim pro necessitate vel utilitate ecclesiae mutilantur et laxantur praecepta canonica."[20] It is to be borne in mind, however, that in these early times any relaxation whatever of the law, whether by absolution or derogation or exception, was considered a dispensation since no canonist had yet given a strict juridical definition of the term.[21]

[15] Thiel, *Epistolae Genuinae Romanorum Pontificum,* t. I, p. 362.

[16] *Bullarium Romanum,* I, p. 41; Mansi II, 702.

[17] Thomassinus, *Vetus et Nova Ecclesiae Disciplina,* t. II, pars 2, L. III, c. 26.

[18] Wernz, *Jus Decretalium* I. tit. IV, n. 121; Stiegler, *Dispensation, Dispensationswesen und Dispensationsrecht,* p. 49.

[19] Cicognani, *Commentarium ad Librum I, Codicis,* p. 316; Cocchi, *Commentarium in Codicem Juris Canonici,* L. I, n. 126.

[20] C. 23, C. I, q. 7.

[21] Brys, *De Dispensatione in Jure Canonico,* p. 16.

CHAPTER IV

THE DEVELOPMENT OF DISPENSATION FROM THE LAW

Article I. To the Time of Gratian

Toward the close of the ninth century a more definite place in canonical works began to be accorded the doctrine of dispensation. Previously it had received only incidental treatment being bound up for the most part with the reconciliation of penitents. In the canonical treatises, however, appearing at this time a more detailed discussion was given over to the doctrine of dispensation as it was then understood among the canonists. But as yet the strict juridical notion of the term had not been agreed upon.[1]

Even until the time of Gratian little of juridical value had been added to the doctrine of dispensation. Gratian himself did not depart from the accepted notion of the term since he was content to define dispensation simply as "the relaxation of the rigor of discipline from mercy." [2] He did however approach somewhat to the juridical exactness of the term perfected after his time when he stated that the rigor of the canon can sometimes be relaxed for a (particular) person.[3]

That Gratian gave serious thought to the possibility of dispensation being a strict juridic entity is clear from his method of treating the term. Unlike Ivo of Chartres who comments on the word only in the prologue to his collection,[4] Gratian embodies the doctrine within his collection.

Article II. Rufinus and the Juridical Definition of Dispensation

While all the early legal minds were attempting to crystallize the term dispensation it was not until the year 1159 that Rufinus finally

[1] *Cf.* Brys, *De Dispensatione in Jure Canonico,* p. 43.

[2] *Dictum Gratiani,* c. 5, C. I, q. 7.

[3] *Cf.* c. 11, C. I, q. 7.

[4] *MPL.,* t. 161, col. 51.

gave a satisfactory and complete legal status to the word.[5] Until the time of Rufinus all the jurists, including Gratian, had been accustomed to regard dispensation in the light of any mutation of the law whether by abrogation or derogation or exception.[6] Rufinus, however, defined dispensation as: "Est itaque dispensatio, justa causa faciente ab eo cujus interest canonici rigoris causalis facta derogatio."

A textual criticism of this definition will serve to indicate that Rufinus had a definite idea of dispensation which was so exacting as to be a decided departure from the notions of those canonists who preceded him.

In the first place he calls dispensation a "derogatio" but here derogation is to be taken in the sense of "relaxatio" [7] and not in the sense of a partial abrogation.[8] This relaxation was to temper the rigor of the law, that is, the canons. Gratian himself admitted this possibility when he made the canons of the Councils and the decrees of the Pontiffs equal in so far as the norms of general ecclesiastical laws were concerned [9] and since they were equal they could all be subject to a "relaxatio." [10] Moreover this relaxation was *causalis*, that is, not general but particular. A derogation is general when the law in whole or in part is taken away from the whole community; it is *causalis* when the obligation of the law is taken away for certain persons or circumstances while the law remains in all its rigor for other persons or other circumstances.[11]

By the words "ab eo cujus interest facta" Rufinus determines the author of dispensation; but he does not further determine who should have this authority.

Lastly this relaxation is brought about by the intervention of a just cause and not simply because of the arbitrary will of the superior.

[5] *Summa Decretorum des Magister Rufinus*, ed. H. Singer, p. 234.

[6] *Cf.* Stiegler, *A. K. K. R.* 1898, p. 91.

[7] *Cf.* Brys, *De Dispensatione in Jure Canonico*, p. 95.

[8] *Cf.* Singer, *Die Summa Decretorum des Magister Rufinus*, p. 14.

[9] C. 2, D. III., in *Dictum Gratiani.*

[10] C. 11, C. I, q. 7.

[11] *Cf.* Brys, *De Dispensatione in Jure Canonico*, p. 96.

Although Rufinus was definite in his notion of dispensation he did not always confine its use to the strict interpretation of the term. To mention one instance,[12] he placed, under the term of dispensation, a mutation of a law which had been introduced because of changed circumstances. It is possible to conclude that Rufinus used the word dispensation in a twofold sense, namely, in a strictly juridical sense and in a broad sense.[13] This fact, however, is of small importance for by his definition of dispensation Rufinus departed from the broad usage of the term and through a juridical formula interpreted for the first time a practice long existent. For several centuries dispensation, that is, the relaxation of a law in a particular case, had existed but it existed under the guise of derogation and abrogation and exception. Rufinus, then, was the first canonist to recognize that dispensation was a distinct legal entity that should be placed within the confines of a strict juridical formula.[14]

On the definition of dispensation advanced by Rufinus in the twelfth century the canonists of succeeding centuries have founded the modern concept of the term. Since the time of Decretalists dispensation has ever remained in law the relaxation of law in a particular case. The concept of dispensation has changed only in so far as more minute juristic elements have been injected into the detailed meaning of the term. This has come about because the science of canonical jurisprudence did not remain fixed with the passing of the legal minds of the period of the Decretalists.

[12] *Cf.* Singer, *Die Summa Decretorum des Magister Rufinus,* ad D. LVIII, p. 150.

[13] *Cf.* Stiegler, *A. K. K. R.*, 1898, p. 102.

[14] *Cf.* Brys, *De Dispensatione in Jure Canonico*, p. 95.

CHAPTER V

THE CAUSE FOR MATRIMONIAL DISPENSATIONS

Article I. The Historical Insistence on the Canonical Cause

While there are disputes among the canonists and historians concerning the fact, the author and the mode of dispensation, all are agreed that dispensations of which there is a record were granted only for a just cause and for the utility and necessity of the Church. In reviewing the history of dispensation during the early centuries it is found that abrogations, exemptions, mutations, in a word dispensations in the then-accepted sense of the term, were granted, not at the will of the superior and not for any cause whatever, but only for a cause, which, because of the necessity or the circumstances of the times, would be of practical value to the whole Church. Even in the instances in which the prohibiting laws of the Councils were relaxed in favor of determined persons it was made certain that these relaxations would redound to the public good of the Church.[1]

Until the period of the Decretalists it seems that dispensations were granted only by reason of a public cause. Gratian seems to have considered the possibility of dispensation for a private cause when he speaks of the toleration on the part of the Church "pro persona."[2] But it is only after the time of Rufinus that the use of a private cause for granting a dispensation was admitted. It seems reasonable to assert that the use of the private cause took its being directly from the definition of dispensation as advanced by Rufinus. Previous to the time of this Decretalist, dispensation only in the wide sense was known. Afterward, when dispensation was considered the relaxation of a law in a particular case, there was no further need for demanding a cause of common utility or necessity since a cause of particular or private necessity would suffice provided

[1] Thomassinus, *Vetus et Nova Ecclesiae Disciplina,* T. II, pars 2, L. III, c. 24.

[2] C. 11, C. I, q. 7.

it redounded indirectly to the utility of the Church.[3] All the Decretalists, however, were not so liberal in their views. The foremost of these, Huguccio, demanded a *causa magna* and this only for public utility.[4]

In continuing the constant tradition of the Church the Council of Trent, in treating of dispensations insisted that a cause must be present for the valid granting of a dispensation.[5] The most recent manifestation of this tradition is to be found in the Code when it is stated that a dispensation from an ecclesiastical law is not to be granted without a just and reasonable cause.[6]

This brief résumé is set forth to indicate that from the time when a mutation of a law was first considered in the Church the cause for the change was the first consideration. If a law is enacted for a special reason or contingency, it follows that such a law should be dispensed from only for a likewise special reason or contingency. In a later chapter the importance of the cause in effecting the liceity and validity of a dispensation will be treated.

Article II. The Juridical Origin of the Canonical Cause

It is the intention of the legislator to make a law for the common good but circumstances often arise which demand the relaxation of a law in a particular case. Because a law is for the common good it cannot be removed or its binding force cannot be relaxed arbitrarily. A notable and worthy reason is necessary in order that the effect of the law may be relaxed in the case where its observance would be difficult or contrary to the common good. This reason in juridical language is called a "cause" and a "cause" which the Church holds as sufficient and for which she grants a dispensation is called a "canonical cause."[7] Primarily a canonical cause regards the public necessity and utility of the Church. But this does not mean that a cause must be directly referred to the common good;

[3] *Cf.* Brys, *De Dispensatione in Jure Canonico,* p. 119.

[4] Huguccio, Cod. ms. cit. fol. 125, col. 1, apud Brys, *De Dispensatione in Jure Canonico,* p. 119.

[5] *Cf.* Conc. Trid., sess. XXV, *de ref.,* c. 8; sess. XXIV, *de ref. matr.,* c. 5.

[6] Canon 84, § 1.

[7] Corradus, *Praxis Dispensationum Apostolicarum* L. I, c. 1, n. 12.

it suffices that the cause influences the common good only indirectly since the good of the part redounds to the good of the whole.[8]

There is no way of knowing exactly the canonical cause during the first nine centuries since the canonists themselves had no clear canonical idea either of the term of dispensation or relaxation or of the cause on which it could be based. A vague description of a canonical cause can be found in a letter written in the year 501 by Pope Symmachus to Avitus, bishop of Vienna, when he says that, "on account of some good the rigor of the law can be relaxed, for which the law itself would have provided if it had been foreseen it (*i. e.,* the good)." [9] In a general way it must be said that relaxations from the law were granted only when the necessity or the public utility of the Church demanded such an action.

To Gratian can probably be ascribed the first list of canonical causes and in exploring the canonical history of the first few centuries he brings forth instances to which he applies his canonical causes for relaxing a law. He states this principle of relaxation in the words: "Nisi rigor disciplinae quandoque relaxetur ex dispensatione misericordiae. Multorum enim crimina sunt damnabilia, quae tamen Ecclesia tolerat pro tempore, pro persona, intuitu pietatis, vel necessitatis, sive utilitatis, et pro eventu rei." [10] At the first glance Gratian seems rather to refer to the toleration of the Church in regard to certain crimes, but, in his application of the causes he enumerates, crimes are not present but rather the modification of some ancient canon of the Fathers or of the Councils. If Gratian had any intention of compiling a list of causes which in modern curial practice would be called canonical causes it can be said that in general the canonical causes for dispensations in the early centuries were public utility and public necessity to the Church and that *in specie* dispensations could be granted by reason of the times [11] or of the person [12] or in the interest of piety [13]

[8] *Cf.* Brys, *De Dispensatione in Jure Canonico,* p. 119.

[9] Thiel, *Epistolae Romanorum Pontificum Genuinae,* p. 657.

[10] C. 5, C. I, q. 7, in *Dictum Gratiani.*

[11] C. 6, C. I, q. 7.

[12] C. 11, C. I, q. 7, in *Dictum Gratiani.*

[13] Conc. Romanum, a. 465, Canon 2—Mansi VII, 961; C. 12, C. I, q. 7, in *Dictum Gratiani.*

or necessity [14] or utility [15] or because of an event that has already transpired.[16]

A conclusion can be drawn from these six causes advanced by Gratian. All through the centuries the canonical causes that have been approved at various times by the *stylus curiae* of the Holy See find a direct relationship to those causes formulated in the twelfth century by Gratian. The doctrine of dispensation has developed but the causes for which dispensations have been granted have remained fundamentally the same. These causes have passed through changes only in the manner in which they have been applied and the persons and the circumstances to which they have been attached during the various periods in canonical history.

Article III. The Historical Background of Certain Canonical Causes

On May 9, 1877, the Sacred Congregation for the Propagation of the Faith compiled a list of canonical causes for matrimonial dispensations. This list contained sixteen causes.[17] In 1901 the Apostolic Dataria compiled a more elaborate list containing twenty-eight causes.[18] For the present only those causes enumerated in the instruction of the Propaganda will be considered. Most of these causes are by no means of recent origin since their use can be traced back for several centuries and are to be found among the works of the leading canonists of the sixteenth and seventeenth centuries.[19]

For the purpose of ascertaining historically the existence of these causes a brief historical summary of each cause will be given. The

[14] C. 13, C. I, q. 7, in *Dictum Gratiani.*

[15] C. 17, C. I, q. 7, in *Dictum Gratiani.*

[16] C. 18, C. I, q. 7, in *Dictum Gratiani.*

[17] S. C. P. F., Instruction, 9 May, 1877—*Collect. P. F.*, n. 1470.

[18] Ex S. Dataria Apostolica—Causae Canonicae Ordinariae Matrimonialium, dispensationum sufficientes sive conjunctae plures sive solae et aliarum normae. *A. S. S.*, XXXIV, p. 34.

[19] De Justis, *De Dispensationibus Matrimonialibus,* L. III; Corradus, *Praxis Dispensationum Apostolicarum,* L. VII et VIII; Sanchez, *De Matrimonio,* L. VIII.

canonical requirements for their application will be dealt with in a later chapter.

These causes are as follows:

1. Narrowness of Place (Angustia Loci)

The origin of this cause is indefinite but it was Paul V (1605-1621) who restricted the use of it to communities having no more than three hundred hearths or fifteen hundred inhabitants.[20] From this fact it can only be argued that if the use of this cause was restricted by Paul V, the origin of the cause must be prior to his time.

As far back as the use of this cause can be traced it is found that it can be invoked when a woman is related within the forbidden degree of consanguinity or affinity to most of the men in the community. If she is to contract marriage she would have to seek one inferior to her in birth, wealth, education, or customs, or she would be forced to leave her home to seek marriage outside her family. In virtue of this cause dispensations have always been granted for a woman to choose a suitable husband from among her relatives.

The origin of this canonical clause could lie in a twofold reason: First, the marriage of persons who are unequal, whether as to age or station, has always been discouraged by the Church; [21] secondly, the Church seems to be not unmindful of the sentiments of Plato and the Latin poets who held that love of country conquers all since all the early canonists agree that a dispensation can be given because of smallness of place lest a woman should be forced to leave her country or even her immediate neighborhood to find a husband who is not related to her.[22]

For several centuries absolute and relative *angustia loci* has been recognized. Absolute *angustia loci* is had by reason of the small size of the place considered in itself. The cause of *angustia loci* could be relatively verified if, even in a populous city, a woman, because of her nationality or high rank, could not find a marriageable equal. Pope Innocent X (1644-55) recognized relative *angustia loci,*

[20] De Justis, *De Dispensationibus Matrimonialibus,* L. III, c. 2.

[21] Corradus, *Praxis Dispensationum Apostolicarum,* L. VII, c. 4, n. 47, 48.

[22] Sanchez, *De Sancto Matrimonii Sacramento,* L. VIII, disput. 19, n. 13.

when he conceded dispensations to nobles provided that in their town or city there were no more than ten noble families.[23]

That this cause of *angustia loci* was one of serious moment especially in the sixteenth and seventeenth centuries is clear from the interesting and minute discussions the authors of the period indulged in regarding its application. They were very definite in classifying nobles into grades for they noted three orders of nobility: that acquired through birth, that acquired through one's own merit, and that obtained through the favor of those in authority. In this last class were to be found the *litterati* and the doctors of the law. A doctor, particularly of canon law, was to be preferred to an inferior nobleman because the nobility acquired through learning and science was held in higher esteem than the obscure nobility acquired through birth.[24]

2. *Superadult Age. (Aetas super adulta)*

The origin of this cause is quite indefinite since the authors simply mention it without further comment. It can be remarked, historically, that until the pontificate of Paul V (1605-1621) the cause of *aetas super adulta* was admitted as frequently as was the cause of *angustia loci.*[25] From this fact it can simply be argued that the origin of this cause antedates the reign of Paul V.

3. *Lack of Proper Dowry. (Deficientia aut incompetentia dotis)*

The origin of the dowry extends into antiquity. Plutarch says that the legislators, Solon and Licurgus would not sanction laws making the dowry an essential to marriage although they were fearful that the undowered woman would remain unmarried. But later the Romans conceived the idea of having the woman dowered (for previously the dower had been furnished by the man) so that the man could marry his equal and the woman would be able to share in the burdens of the married state. This idea of the dowry, however, did not pertain in any way to the essence of marriage; but

[23] Corradus, *Praxis Dispensationum Apostolicarum,* L. VII, c. 5, n. 45.

[24] De Justis, *De Dispensationibus Matrimonialibus,* L. III, c. 2, n. 51.

[25] Corradus, *Praxis Dispensationum Apostolicarum,* L. VII, c. 2, n. 83-85.

because of the burdens arising from the married state, it was difficult for men to accept undowered wives.[26]

In the Council of Arles (a. 524) it was decreed that there should be no marriage without a dowry [27] but Fontanella says that little attention was given to this decree.[28] But whenever it could possibly be done, parents dowered their daughters. In fact in some places wealthy parents so vied with one another in settling dowries on their daughters that this became a source of scandal. To counteract this evil a law was enacted in Venice in the sixteenth century fixing the maximum of the dowry at six thousand gold ducats. In many places the dower tax existed and in some instances, particularly in Castile, the origin of the dower tax goes back into antiquity while in Catalonia the Curia taxed the dowry as early as 1599.[29]

4. *Legal Litigation Already Begun With Regard to an Inheritance. (Lites de bonis)*

The natural origin of this cause lies in the constant anxiety of the Church to preserve peace or to restore it as quickly as possible when it has been disturbed.[30] Nothing much can be said concerning the historical background of this cause. By way of example it can, however, be stated that Alexander VII (1655-1657) granted a dispensation for such a cause in the second degree of consanguinity.[31] Even earlier Urban VIII (1623-1644) granted a dispensation for this cause in a closer degree of consanquinity because in this particular instance the lawsuit caused such intense hatred that there was danger to life.[32]

5. *Poverty of a Widow (Paupertas viduae)*

This cause was found among those listed by the canonists of the

[26] Fontanella, *De Pactis Nuptialibus,* I, II, clausula 5, Glos. 1, pars 1.
[27] C. 6, C. XXX, q. 5.
[28] Fontanella, *De Pactis Nuptialibus,* I, II, clausula 5, Glos. 1, pars 1.
[29] Fontanella, *De Pactis Nuptialibus,* I, II, clausula 5, Glos. 1, pars 1.
[30] C. 2, *de judiciis,* II, 2 in Clem.
[31] Corradus, *Praxis Dispensationum Apostolicarum,* L. VII, c. 2, n. 64.
[32] Corradus, *Praxis Dispensationum Apostolicarum,* L. VII, c. 2, n. 66.

sixteenth and seventeenth centuries and was accepted in the curial practice of those times.[83] It is difficult to determine the origin of this cause for in the works of the classical canonists of that day the cause is simply mentioned without further comment. The basis of the cause probably lies in the fact that the Church, in her desire to provide for the spiritual and temporal welfare of the children of widows, was willing to grant matrimonial dispensations, on the strength of this cause, to widowed mothers who found it difficult to give their minor children the proper care if they remained in their widowhood.

6. The Advantage of Peace (Bonum Pacis)

The Church has always been most desirous of restoring peace and it has always been her policy to adopt the quickest measures that peace might be restored.[84] It is not strange, then, that the early canonists would consider the preservation of peace as being a worthy canonical cause. It would be difficult to determine when this cause was first admitted in curial practice but it can be stated historically that Pope Nicholas II (1059-1061) went so far as to permit the marriages of children when such marriages in royal families would bring or assure peace to given localities.[85] It is of further interest to note that one of the first recorded instances of papal dispensation for contracting marriage in the forbidden degrees was granted for the cause of peace. In this instance Innocent III (1198-1216) permitted the marriage of Otto IV with the daughter of the Duke of Suabia, they being related in the fourth degree of consanguinity in the collateral line. This dispensation was granted that peace might be restored between the warring kingdoms of Germany and Suabia.[86]

7. Carnal Intercourse Among Relatives and Subsequent Pregnancy. (Copula et praegnantia)

Although this cause is listed by the Propaganda it was considered as a cause by the classical authors only when conception took place

[83] Corradus, *Praxis Dispensationum Apostolicarum,* L. VII, c. 2.
[84] C. 2, *de judiciis,* II, 2, in Clem.
[85] C. 2, *de dispensatione impuberum,* IV, 2.
[86] Lupus, *Opera Omnia Canonica,* t. IV, p. 188.

between relatives in good faith. In the opinion of Sanchez, pregnancy resulting from the crime of incest did not constitute a just cause for the Superior to dispense.[37]

8. Evil Repute of the Woman. (Infamia mulieris)

Little of historical interest can be found concerning this cause. It appears frequently in the writings of the classical canonists and was introduced into curial practice as a canonical cause by Pope Paul V (1605-1621).[38]

9. Revalidation of a Marriage Contracted in Good Faith With Ignorance of an Impediment. (Revalidatio matrimonii)

The basis of this cause is found in the good faith of the parties contracting and the scandal which customarily arises from the dissolution of the putative marriage. Reputable canonists since the Council of Trent have admitted its use.[39]

10. The Removal of Grave Scandals. (Remotio gravium scandalorum)

Scandal has always been a just cause for dispensing in every forbidden case and, conversely, if scandal would arise from the concession of the dispensation it should by no means be granted.[40] Very early in her history the Church recognized that the avoidance of scandal was a just cause in the granting of dispensations. With this thought in mind Gratian remarks that "lest there would be too much scandal in the Church," Pope Innocent I in 414 received into the ranks of the clergy those clerics who had been ordained by the heretical Bonosus.[41]

[37] *Cf.* Sanchez, *De Matrimonio,* L. VIII, disput. 19, n. 33.

[38] Corradus, *Praxis Dispensationum Apostolicarum,* L. VIII, c. 1.

[39] Sanchez, *De Matrimonio,* L. VIII, disput. 19, n. 33; De Justis, *De Dispensationibus Matrimonialibus,* L. III, c. 16 Corradus, *Praxis Dispensationum Apostolicarum,* L. VII, c. 3.

[40] Corradus, *Praxis Dispensationum Apostolicarum,* L. VII, c. 2.

[41] C. 6, C. I, q. 7.

11. Excellence of Merits. (Excellentia meritorium)

The Scriptures can be invoked to trace the origin of this canonical cause. In speaking of the healing of the centurion's son, St. Luke records that the Jewish ancients said to Jesus: "He is worthy that Thou shouldst do this for him."[42] The Church has always been most generous in granting favors to those who are worthy of her kindness. It would be impossible to fix the time when a dispensation was first given by reason of this cause but as an historical fact it can be noted that Urban VIII in 1642 granted a dispensation permitting the marriage of John of Sanseverino and Dalia of Sanseverino, they being related in the second degree of consanguinity. This family was in papal favor because of its prominence and because of the aid it had given to the Holy See.[43]

To the foregoing eleven causes found with more or less similarity among the authors of the sixteenth and seventeenth centuries the Propaganda has added five other causes, bringing the total to sixteen. Four of these causes could have an historical association with those listed in the older authors. These may have been omitted in the past because the authors considered them already comprehended by the other causes. They may have been listed by the Propaganda as separate causes because this Congregation wishes to draw finer distinctions in their application. The fifth cause, that is, dangerous familiarity, is a cause originating in the instruction of the Propaganda.

The two causes, danger of a mixed marriage or of a marriage contracted before a non-Catholic minister—and danger of a civil marriage can be traced historically to the causes "For Belgium" and "For Germany" found among the older authors.[44] The Pope was prompted to grant dispensation in Belgium and Germany because of the predominance of heretics living in these regions. Today the danger of civil and mixed marriage is ever present because of the predominance of heretics in our own country. These causes moreover, ad-

[42] Luke VII, 4.

[43] Corradus, *Praxis Dispensationum Apostolicarum*, L. VII, c. 2, n. 110.

[44] Corradus, *Praxis Dispensationum Apostolicarum*, L. VII, c. 2, n. 96.

vanced by the Propaganda have their foundation in the common danger of scandal together with the danger of perversion or apostasy which could result from either civil or mixed marriages.

The causes of cessation of public concubinage and danger of incestuous concubinage find their common basis in the desire of the Church to avert and remove scandal for concubinage or even its near occasion can give rise to scandal. It would seem that the classical authors comprehended these two causes in the cause of removal of scandal.

The fifth addition that the Propaganda has made, namely, danger of familiarity, originates in the instruction of this Congregation. This seems quite certain for the authors who wrote prior to the publication of the instruction make no mention of such a cause. This observation is of slight importance however, since the absence of such a cause among the lists compiled by previous authors would not indicate that the cause was not admitted in curial practice prior to the instruction of the Propaganda. All such lists are given only *demonstrative.*

PART III

CANONICAL COMMENTARY

CHAPTER VI

THE CAUSE IN DISPENSATORY ACTS

Article I. The Importance of the Cause

Canon 84, § 1—"A lege ecclesiastica ne dispensetur sine justa rationabili causa, . . . ; alias dispensatio ab inferiore data illicita et invalida est."

Two elements are necessary for a dispensation, namely, the power to dispense and the cause for dispensing.[1] The dispensatory powers of the Pope and of bishops, priests and confessors has already been noted. Attention now will be directed toward the cause necessary for dispensation. Aside from the power of the proper authority to dispense it should be noted that the other most important single element in the notion of dispensation is the cause. The presence of the cause can determine the validity or invalidity of any dispensation excepting those cases mentioned in Canons 45 and 1054 which exceptions will be treated more fully later. Furthermore, the cause is an element independent of the power of the one dispensing. In other words, it is a complement of and not a consequence of the power of the one dispensing, for the one dispensing, excluding the legislator, may have the power to dispense but may not be able to exercise it in a given case unless a cause is present. In the doctrine of dispensation the necessity of a cause always has been stressed.[2]

[1] *Cf.* Giovine, *De Dispensationibus Matrimonialibus,* I, Consult. IV, LXIII, n. 1.

[2] Thomassinus, *Vetus et Nova Ecclesiae Disciplina* Tom. II, pars 2, L. III, c. 24, c. 5, C. I., q. 7, *in Dictum Gratiani* Liber de excommunicatis vitandis in Mon. German Hist., *Libelli De Lite,* t. II, p .141; *Summa Decretorum des Magister Rufinus,* ed. H. Singer, p. 234; Sanctus Bernardus, *De Consideratione,* L. III, c. 4; *Opera Omnia;* Conc. Trident., sess. XXIV, *de ref. matr.,* c. 5; sess. XXV, *de ref.,* C. 8; Benedict XIV, ep. encycl., *"Inter omnigenas,"* 2 February, 1744, II, 25, *Fontes,* n. 337; *Codex Juris Canonici,* Canon 84, § 1.

The purpose here will be to demonstrate the necessity and the practical importance and value of the cause in regard to the granting of matrimonial dispensations through the diocesan curia.

1. *The Cause in Relation to Papal Dispensation*

Through ordinary power the Roman Pontiff can dispense from all ecclesiastical laws, whether these have been made by himself, by his predecessors, by general Councils or by the Apostles as bishops of the early Church.[3] He is superior to all ecclesiastical laws and he stands as the supreme legislator for the whole Church. Since the legislator has the power to make laws, he likewise has the power to dispense from them according to the principle: "Omnis res per quascumque causas nascitur, per easdem dissolvitur." [4] But even though the Pope is the supreme legislator and can dispense from every ecclesiastical law, the absence of a cause for dispensing will somewhat place a limitation on his dispensatory acts. This limitation, however, regards only the liceity of his acts for by Canon 84, § 1, a just and proportionate cause is necessary for the liceity of every dispensation, not only when an inferior dispenses in the law of a superior, but also when the legislator, even though he should be the Roman Pontiff, dispenses in his own law. The reasonableness of this principle is evident. Law is an ordination of reason; but it would be unreasonable for the legislator, of his own volition and without cause, to disrupt this ordination or reason which has been established for the common good.[5]

The presence of a just cause, however, is not necessary for the

[3] C. 16, C. XXV, q. I, *in Dictum Gratiani;* Reg. Juris, 46 in VI°: "Is qui in jus succedit alterius, eo jure, quo ille, uti debebit." Sixtus IV, bulla, *"Licet ea,"* 9 August 1479, prop. 7, Errores Petri de Osma, damn: "Papa non potest dispensare in statutis universalis Ecclesiae." Denz.-Bannw., n. 731; Benedict XIV, Const., *"Magnae nobis,"* 29 Junii, 1748—*Fontes,* n. 387; Suarez, *Tractatus De Legibus,* L. VI, c. 14, n. 2; Reiffenstuel, *Jus Canonicum Universum,* Tom. IV, Append. de Disp. super Imped. matr., C. I, n. I; S. Thomas, *Quodlib,* IV, a 13; Codex Juris Canonici, Canon 81.

[4] C. 1, X, *de regulis juris,* VI, 41.

[5] *Cf.* Michiels, *Normae Generales,* II, pp. 499, 500. Sanctus Bernardus, *De Consideratione,* L. III, c. 4, n. 18; *Opera Omnia,* Tom. III, p. 60.

validity of a dispensatory act of the Roman Pontiff. According to a most common opinion among canonists it is held that a dispensation granted without a just cause by a legislator from his own law or by a successor in the law of his predecessor, or by a superior in the law of an inferior, is valid.[6] This principle is based on the notion that the entire obligatory force of law depends on the will of the legislator.[7] The Pope, therefore, in dispensing from any ecclesiastical law without a just cause, acts validly.

In theory it can well be said that the Roman Pontiff can dispense validly from any ecclesiastical law without a just cause.[8] In practice, however, this theory is never borne out for it has been the constant tradition in the Church that the Roman Pontiffs have hesitated to dispense without cause, lest they should act illicitly. That this is true is clear from the fact that whenever any utterance concerning dispensations issues from the Pope, whether through councils or constitutions or letters or grants of faculties through congregations, he insists that dispensations never must be granted unless a just cause is present.[9]

2. *The Cause in Relation to Episcopal Dispensation*

It has been seen that when the Pope dispenses from any ecclesiastical law the presence of the just cause is necessary only for the liceity of his dispensatory acts. When a bishop dispenses from any general ecclesiastical law the presence of the just cause is necessary for the *validity* of the dispensation which he grants, except under

[6] Suarez, *Tractatus De Legibus*, L. VI, c. 14, n. 6; Reiffenstuel, *Jus Canonicum Universum*, L. I, tit. 2, XVIII, n. 479; Benedictus XIV, *De Synodo Diocesana*, L. XIII, c. 5.

[7] *Cf.* Michiels, *Normae Generales*, II, p. 501.

[8] *Cf.* Benedictus XIV, *De Synodo Diocesana*, L. XIII, c. 5, n. 7; Corradus, *Praxis Dispensationum Apostolicarum*, L. VIII, c. 3; Sanchez, *De Matrimonio*, L. VIII, disput. 17, n. 4.

[9] *Cf.* Conc. Trident; sess. XXIV, *de ref. matr.*, c. 5; sess. XXV, *de ref.*, c. 8; Benedictus XIV, *De Synodo Diocesana*, XIII, c. 5, n. 7; S. C. de Prop. F., litt. encycl., 11 Mart., 1868—*Collect.*, n. 1324; S. C. de Prop. F., Instr., 9 Maii, 1877—*Collect.*, n. 1470.

certain conditions provided by law.[10] When the bishop grants dispensations from matrimonial impediments through force of his habitual faculties he acts through power conceded to him. There are instances, however, according to some authors[11] when the bishop dispenses through *ordinary* power, from matrimonial impediments, namely when he dispenses in virtue of Canons 81, 1043 and 1045. On the other hand there are authors who hold that when a bishop dispenses in virtue of these canons he is acting through power *delegated* by law.[12] It will be of no practical value here to attempt to determine whether or not Canons 81, 1043 and 1045 confer powers ordinary or delegated *a jure* on the bishop since the purpose of this thesis is to comment on the *cause* for dispensation. The point to be noted here lies in the fact that for the most part the bishop grants matrimonial dispensations through force of the habitual faculties conceded to him either by the Sacred Consistorial Congregation or by the Sacred Congregation of the Propagation of the Faith, together with the powers he receives through Canons 81, 1043 and 1045.[13]

Matrimonial impediments are governed by the general laws of the Church[14] and when a bishop dispenses from any matrimonial impediment he is an inferior dispensing in the law of a superior and hence must be governed by the principle:

A dispensation granted without a just cause by an inferior in the law of a superior is not only illicit but is invalid.

This principle is a common teaching among canonists.[15] This is no theoretical assumption but it is one borne out in practice. It has been noted already that since the Pope himself is so careful in insisting on the presence of a cause for dispensing regardless of the fact

[10] Canon 1054.

[11] *Cf.* Sanchez, *De Matrimonio,* L. II, disput. 40, n. 14; S. Alphonsus, *Theologia Moralis,* L. VI, n. 1125 et L. VII, n. 93; Gasparri, *Tractatus Canonicus de Matrimonio* (1904) I, n. 444; Michiels, *Normae Generales,* II, p. 469.

[12] *Cf.* Fuster, *Jus Pontificium,* 1923, p. 44; Ojetti, *De natura potestatis Ordinariorum secundum Codicem,* in Gregorianum VI, pp. 436-441.

[13] *Cf.* Canons 248, 252.

[14] Canon 1038.

[15] *Cf.* Sanchez, *De Matrimonio,* L. III, disput. 17, n. 4; Reiffenstuel, *Jus Canonicum Universum,* L. I, XVIII, n. 463 sq.; De Justis, *De Dispensationibus Matrimonialibus,* L. II, c. 2, n. 49; L. III, c. 1, n. 15—Canon 84, § 1.

that he can validly act without a cause, it is only natural that one inferior to the Pope, namely the bishop, must dispense only when a just cause is present.

In granting a matrimonial dispensation, therefore, the bishop is dispensing in the law of a superior and hence to act validly he must have a just and legitimate cause.[16] The obligation of ascertaining the presence and justice of the cause is placed on the one who grants the dispensation.[17] Through force of circumstance the bishop must rely on the pastor to establish the presence of the just cause. The validity or invalidity of a dispensation, provided the impediment involved is a major impediment, can therefore be attributed to the diligence or carelessness of the pastor since he, rather than the bishop, is in a better position to know whether the cause alleged really exists. He has an obligation, then, in conscience, to make certain as to the existence of the cause alleged and then it is for the bishop himself to determine the justice and reasonableness of the cause.

Article II. The Quality of the Cause Necessary for Dispensatory Acts

Canon 84, § 1—"A lege ecclesiastica ne dispensetur sine justa et rationabili causa, habita ratione gravitatis legis a qua dispensatur, . . . "

The cause common to dispensation in general is of a twofold nature, namely, the motivating or final cause[18] and the impulsive

[16] *Cf.* Canon 84, § 1.

[17] Benedictus XIV, const. *"Ad Apostolicae,"* 25 February, 1742, 2: "Sane quidem ad dispensationes obtinendas, an iis, qui eas postulant, in supplici libello causae pro illis consequendis exprimi solent; quae si eiusmodi fuerint, ut juxta canonicas Sanctiones, et prudens Ecclesiasticae Provisionis arbitrium, locus ad dispensandum esse videatur, dispensatio concedi solet, eiusque executio Ordinario, ut plurimum committi; an causae expositae veritate nitantur, ut, veris illis existentibus, gratia executioni demandetur, secus vero, si causae nullatenus veritati consentaneae sint."

[18] *Cf.* Canon 42, § 2; Canon 45.

cause. The motivating or final cause is that cause which, in itself, is capable of inducing the superior to grant the dispensation which is being sought. The impulsive cause is that cause which lends added weight to the final cause.[19]

The final and impulsive cause, in connection with the law from which dispensation is being sought, can be either intrinsic or extrinsic. An intrinsic cause (either final or impulsive) is a cause which is directly opposed to a determined law. In other words it is a certain difficulty or inconvenience which *per accidens* is connected to the observance of the law and which renders this particular law onerous. For example, the necessity of marrying at once that a journey might be begun offers an intrinsic cause for dispensing from the publication of the banns.

An extrinsic cause (likewise either final or impulsive) is a cause which does not come directly from the difficulty of observing a law in a particular case but rather it arises from a certain good to be obtained through the relaxation of some particular law. An example of an extrinsic cause would be a threatened or existing scandal which would be averted or repaired if the dispensation sought was granted.[20]

Regarding matrimonial dispensations, the cause is said to be either canonical or noncanonical and these canonical causes can be either honorable or disparaging. When a cause is advanced for a matrimonial dispensation it may be a canonical cause, so-called, but aside from this it will be either final or impulsive according to the value the one dispensing places on it, for in the last analysis it is left to the prudent judgment of the one dispensing to determine whether or not the cause advanced is worthy or unworthy.[21] If the cause advanced in the petition for a particular matrimonial dispensation does not happen to be one of the so-called canonical causes

[19] *Cf.* Reiffenstuel, *Jus Canonicum Universum*, L. I, lit. 3, n. 194; Sanchez, *De Matrimonio*, L. VIII, disput. 21, n. 41; De Justis, *De Dispensationibus Matrimonialibus*, L. III, c. I, n. 46; Chelodi, *Jus De Personis*, n. 78; Payen, *De Matrimonio*, III, n. 727.

[20] *Cf.* Suarez, *Tractatus De Legibus*, L. VI, c. 18, n. 26; Cappello, *De Sacramentis*, I, n. 133, ad 7; Sipos, *Enchiridion Juris Canonici*, p 26; Michiels, *Normae Generales*, II, p. 503.

[21] *Cf.* Michiels, *Normae Generales*, II, p. 504.

found, for example in the Instruction of the Propaganda, it may be, however, of value in the dispensatory act under consideration.

Since the lists of canonical causes which have originated from various sources [22] are only demonstrative, it must follow that other causes could be possible for the granting of matrimonial dispensations. Schmalzgrueber has attempted to describe in general a sufficient cause for a matrimonial dispensation. He states: "As often as those circumstances are present which, unless the dispensation was granted, would force the woman to remain unmarried or to contract an unequal marriage, and these facts are clear, the cause is sufficient from whatsoever source it may come." [23]. This description is fairly comprehensive but the sufficiency of any cause must be determined first in proportion to the law from which dispensation is being granted and then according to the circumstances which make the law onerous in a particular case.

It will be recalled that Canon 84, § 1, states: "A lege ecclesiastica ne dispensetur sine justa et rationabili causa habita ratione gravitatis legis a qua dispensatur, . . . " The prescription of this canon refers to dispensation from ecclesiastical law in general. Only the justice and reasonableness of the cause necessary for matrimonial dispensations will be regarded here and an attempt will be made to demonstrate the value and necessity of this canon in questions concerning dispensations from matrimonial impediments.

Were the Code to state simply that a just and reasonable cause was necessary for a dispensation it could be claimed that the statute was vague. To strengthen the statement demanding the presence of a just and reasonable cause the Code fixes a determining norm by decreeing that the justice and reasonableness of the cause are to be in proportion to the gravity of the law from which dispensation is sought.

Suarez [24] has formulated a principle somewhat identical to the one formulated in Canon 84, § 1. His principle states: "Ubi fuerit

[22] S. C. P. F., Instruction, 9 May, 1877; *Collect. P. F.*, n. 1470; "Ex S. Dataria Apostolica," *A. S. S.*, XXXIV, pp. 34, 35.

[23] Schmalzgrueber, *Jus Ecclesiasticum Universum*, T. I, pars III, t. 16, n. 129.

[24] Suarez, *Tractatus De Legibus*, L. VI, c. 18, n. 16.

major obligatio, ibi major causa postulatur." It must follow logically, in general, that a greater cause is required for dispensing from the diriment matrimonial impediments than from the merely impeding impediments.[25] This, however, is a rather general statement. It can be seen that a greater and more weighty cause will be necessary for dispensing from the impediment of disparity of cult than from the impediment of legal adoption. But in practice there seems to be no reason for admitting a grave cause in the petition for dispensation from the impeding impediment of mixed religion and for demanding a more grave cause when the impediment involved is that of disparity of cult. In dispensing from these two impediments especially, it is required only that just and grave causes be present for either dispensation.[26] Since the prescriptions governing these two impediments are so definitely joined in the Code,[27] it would seem that in the mind of the Code these two impediments are on a parallel in so far as dispensation from them is concerned. Aside from this practical observation the general principle enunciated by Suarez is to be invoked whenever possible in determining the gravity of the cause in proportion to the gravity of the law from which dispensation is being sought.[28]

ARTICLE III. THE GRADATION IN THE QUALITY OF CAUSE AND THE GRAVITY OF LAW

It will be noted that Canon 84, § 1, uses the phrase, "Habita ratione gravitatis legis a qua dispensatur." By these words it is not meant that the cause considered in itself or *absolutely* is just and reasonable, but the cause must be just and reasonable, according to the gravity of the law from which dispensation is being sought.

[25] *Cf.* Michiels, *Normae Generales*, II, p. 503.

[26] *Cf.* Canons 1061, § 1, n. 1 and 1071. Also, Schenk, *Mixed Religion and Disparity of Cult*, n. 286.

[27] That is, Canon 1071 says that all those provisions surrounding the impediment of mixed religion as found in Canons 1060-1064 are to apply equally to the impediment of disparity of cult.

[28] *"Ubi fuerit major obligatio, ibi major causa postulatur."*—Suarez, *Tractatus De Legibus*, L. VI, c. 18, n. 16.

This would indicate, *a priori,* that in ecclesiastical discipline there exists a definite scale in the quality of causes and it is further indicated that there exists a gradation in the gravity of different laws.[29]

In only two instances, namely, in Canon 1061, § 1, n. 1, and in Canon 1071 does the Code mention specifically the possibility of a *matrimonial dispensation* together with the quality of the cause necessary for such a dispensation. In various other instances, for example, dispensation from the banns, or the reason for which a bishop can temporarily forbid a marriage the Code mentions the quality of the cause in reference to other ecclesiastical prescriptions. This fact is mentioned merely to indicate that in the mind of the Code there is a gradation both in the quality of the cause and in the gravity of various ecclesiastical laws. Since, as was stated above, the Code mentions the possibility of a matrimonial dispensation and the cause necessary for it in only two instances, it will be necessary to go beyond the treatment of matrimonial dispensations in order to indicate more clearly the gradation existing in the quality of causes and the gravity of laws. This fact, however, can be indicated sufficiently by a perusal of the canons on matrimonial legislation in which a cause is required for the fulfillment of the prescriptions indicated in the individual canons.

1. *The Legitimate Cause*

To this end it can be noted that Canon 1028, § 1, permits the local Ordinary, for a *legitimate cause,* to dispense from the publication of the marriage banns even in another diocese. The purpose of the publication of banns is, naturally, to determine more accurately and more certainly the *status liber* of the contracting parties. If the *status liber* of the contractants is certainly known to the Ordinary, this knowledge, in the opinion of St. Alphonsus [30] forms a *causa legitima* sufficient for the Ordinary to dispense from the banns. Ordinarily the bishop will have little difficulty in ascertaining the *status liber* of the contractants and hence, once he has arrived at the

[29] *Cf.* Michiels, *Normae Generales,* II, p. 506.

[30] St. Alphonsus, *Theologia Moralis,* L. 6, 1006.

knowledge that no impediment impedes the proposed marriage, he is not bound to seek further for a grave or a most urgent cause before dispensing from the publication of the banns. In short, the end of the law is to determine the *status liber* of the contractants. When this has been ascertained the end of the law ceases. At that point the law prescribing the publication of the banns presents no great barrier to the proposed marriage and the *causa legitima*, because it is in proportion to the gravity of the law, will suffice for granting the dispensation sought.[31]

2. *The Just Cause*

The cause demanded in Canon 1039, § 1, is described as the *causa justa*. By force of this canon, if a just cause is present and so long as it endures, the bishop can deny, in a particular case and for a definite time, the right to marry to all those living in his territory and his subjects even outside his territory. It is true in this instance the cause herein described is not regarding a dispensation but nevertheless its presence in the canon testifies as to the gradation in the quality of cause and in the gravity of law. In Canon 1035 it is stated that all are able to contract marriage unless they are prohibited by law. A prohibition to marry placed by law, either natural or positive, is called an impediment. According to Canon 1038, § 2, only the supreme authority in the Church can place legal impediments. In particular instances, however, it can happen that a marriage should be forbidden for a time, for example, because the parents of the contractants are opposed to the marriage, or because there is present a prudent suspicion that an impediment is hindering the union, or because there is a real fear that grave harm will arise from the contracting of the marriage.[32] In such circumstances, the prescriptions of Canons 1035 and 1038, § 2, can for a time be suspended. Because a possible harm can be foreseen if these canons are adhered to, their prescriptions, by force of Canon 1039, § 1, become less grave and by reason of a *just cause* (not a grave or most urgent one) these canons for a time can be relaxed.

[31] *Cf.* Cappello, *De Sacramentis,* III, n. 168.

[32] *Cf.* Payen, *De Matrimonio,* I, n. 588.

3. *The Reasonable Cause*

Another gradation of the cause is found in Canon 1030, § 1. Here the cause is described *causa rationabilis*. By force of this canon the pastor should not assist at a marriage until, the banns having been published and an investigation having been made, he has obtained the necessary documents attesting to the baptism of the contractants [33] and to their *status liber*.[34] Having obtained these he should not, furthermore, assist at the marriage until three days have elapsed from the final publication of the banns, unless a reasonable cause demands otherwise. By reason of the first part of this canon when the pastor has obtained the necessary documents the *status liber* of the contractants has been established. This makes the law demanding a delay of three days a less grave one and by placing the cause in proportion to the gravity of the law about which it revolves, the cause excusing from the prescriptions of this less grave law need be only a reasonable cause.

4. *The Just and Reasonable Cause*

Still another description of the cause is had in Canon 1109, § 2. This canon prescribes that in an extraordinary case and for a *just and reasonable cause,* the Ordinary can permit the celebration of the marriage ceremony in private homes.[35] By nature this law need not be adhered to under the strictest conditions and hence it does not seem that it is a *lex gravis*. The cause for excusing from this law, regarded in proportion to the gravity of the law, need not be a grave or urgent one but by force of Canon 1109, § 2, it need be only a just and reasonable one. The quality of this cause mentioned in this canon is on a different scale than the cause mentioned in Canon 1031, § 1. In this latter canon only a reasonable cause was demanded. Since the *status liber* of the contractants had already been established any reasonable cause would excuse from the law demanding an interval of three days before celebrating the marriage. Such a reasonable cause could be,

[33] Canon 1021, § 1.

[34] Canon 1020.

[35] *Cf.* Canon 1109, § 2.

for example, the unwillingness to defer any longer a marriage which had already been delayed beyond the expectations of the contracting parties. In Canon 1109, § 2, however, the cause, aside from being reasonable, must also be just before the Ordinary can permit the celebration of the marriage ceremony in a private home. By way of illustration it might be stated that it could be *reasonable* on the part of the contractants to wish to have the marriage ceremony take place in a certain private home because of the sentimental associations each may have in connection with that home. But the cause would be both *just* and *reasonable,* in accordance with Canon 1109, § 2, if, for example, the contracting parties found it difficult to reach the church.[36]

5. The Just and Grave Cause

It will be more in keeping with the spirit of this dissertation to note the quality of the cause described in Canon 1061, § 1, n. 1. This canon speaks directly of a matrimonial dispensation. By force of this canon it is indicated that the Church will not dispense from the impediment of mixed religion (or disparity of cult, according to Canon 1071) except for a cause that is both *just and grave.* Here it will be well to revert to the phrase found in Canon 84, § 1, *"habita ratione gravitatis legis a qua dispensatur."* There is sufficient connection between these two canons to make the prescription of Canon 1061, § 1, n. 1, self-evident. That the law imposing the impediment of mixed religion (and disparity of cult) is a grave one is clear from the fact that in Canon 1060 it is stated that the Church most severely prohibits the marriages between baptized persons, one party being a Catholic and the other a heretic or schismatic. Furthermore, if such a marriage would be the occasion of offering danger of perversion to the Catholic party and to the children, such a union is forbidden even by the divine law.[37] Hence to excuse from this grave law which imposes such a matrimonial impediment, Canon 84, § 1, must be invoked to remind the one dispensing that a due proportion must exist between the cause and the gravity of the law from which

[36] *Cf.* Vlaming, *Praelectiones Juris Matrimonii,* II, n. 616.

[37] Canon 1060.

dispensation is being sought. With regard to this particular impediment of mixed religion it is stated that a dispensation is not to be granted from it except for a just and grave cause. In virtue of Canon 1061, § 1, n. 1, therefore, it is seen that a legitimate, or a reasonable or a just cause will not suffice. The law from which dispensation is being sought in this particular case is a grave one and in proportion to it the cause for the dispensation must be just and grave.[38]

6. The Most Grave Cause

The cause mentioned in Canon 1063, § 2, is qualified as *causa gravissima.* By force of Canon 1063, § 1, it is forbidden to those who have obtained a dispensation from the impediment of mixed religion, either before or after the marriage has been contracted *coram Ecclesia,* to go before a non-Catholic minister, *qua minister,* and there give or renew their matrimonial consent. In virtue of paragraph 2 of this canon it is prescribed that if the pastor certainly knows that the contractants will violate or already have violated the prescriptions contained in paragraph 1, he must not assist at the marriage unless a most grave cause is present, and unless scandal is removed and the Ordinary has been consulted. The consideration here, as far as this dissertation is concerned, is with the *causa gravissima.* Again it will be well to revert to Canon 84, § 1, and recall that the quality of the cause must be in proportion to the gravity of the law. It is true that Canon 84 regards dispensation. It seems permissable to use this canon for a background in illustrating the existence of a gradation in the quality of cause and the gravity of law. By placing Canon 84, § 1, in juxtaposition to Canon 1063, §§ 1 and 2, it will be seen why the cause mentioned in Canon 1063 is qualified as *causa gravissima.* If the prescriptions of Canon 1063, §§ 1 and 2, are disregarded, the contractants have become, or will become, guilty of *communicatio activa in sacris.*[39] Such an act on the part of Catholics is abhorrent to the mind of the Church.[40] A law forbidding *com-*

[38] *Cf.* Payen, *De Matrimonio,* I, n. 862.

[39] Canon 1258, § 1: "Haud licitum est fidelibus quovis modo active assistere seu partem habere in sacris acatholicorum."

[40] *Cf.* Litt. S. C. S. Off., 17 February, 1864—*Fontes,* n. 976.

municatio in sacris is of necessity a law of grave nature or even of more than grave nature. The cause required for permitting a pastor to act contrary to the prescriptions of Canon 1063, § 1, must be in proportion to the gravity of the enactments of this part of the canon and this proportion is fixed in the second paragraph of the canon where it is stated that only a most grave cause will suffice.

7. *The Most Grave and Most Urgent Cause*

Finally, the quality of the cause mentioned in Canon 1104 is *causa gravissima et urgentissima.* This canon prescribes the conditions under which a marriage of conscience may be permitted. The Church is loath to permit such marriages because "ex natura rei" it is to the best interests of all concerned that marriage should possess not only the recognition of public authority but should also be celebrated publicly.[41] Moreover, a marriage of conscience is followed by certain inconveniences to the contractants themselves, to the children born of the union and to others.[42] The contractants could suffer because although they have the right, scandal being removed, to the use of marriage, they nevertheless are unable to observe the *vitae conjugalis communionem.* Often, too, in some countries a marriage of conscience will work an *incommodum* on the contractants by presenting the danger of polygamy.[43] With regard to the children born of a marriage of conscience it could happen easily that they would be deserted by the parents, or be left unbaptized or be insufficiently educated. Or, since the fact of the marriage of conscience remains secret, it could happen that the children would be regarded as being illegitimate. And finally, the marriage of conscience may be a source of scandal to others. It may happen that the contractants to a marriage of conscience may live most familiarly and this fact would cause others, who were unaware of the existence of a marriage bond between the two, to believe that the parties were *concubinarii.*

[41] *Cf.* Wernz-Vidal, *Jus Matrimoniale,* V, n. 566.

[42] *Cf.* Payen, *De Matrimonio,* II, 1939.

[43] *Cf.* Benedictus XIV, ep. encycl., *Satis Vobis,* 17 November, 1741, §§ 1, 2, 6, 8—*Fontes,* n. 319.

Keeping in mind the possibility of these various *incommoda,* it can be seen that the thought of a marriage of conscience is particularly adverse to the mind of the Church and the prescription forbidding it is a law most grave by nature. The cause excusing from this law must conform to the gravity of the law and hence the cause, according to Benedict XIV,[44] cannot be any cause whatsoever but must be a *"causa gravis, urgens et urgentissima."* The Code has seen fit to more definitely strengthen the cause and demands a *causa gravissima et urgentissima.*[45]

While, as it has been remarked, all the foregoing canons do not deal with the cause for dispensation, nevertheless, it seems in place to note them to explain more completely the phrase used in Canon 84, § 1: *"habita ratione gravitatis legis a qua dispensatur."* From a perusal of these canons it can be deduced that, in the mind of the legislator, some laws are grave and others are more grave. It must follow then, by reason of Canon 84, § 1, the just and reasonable cause must at times be grave and at other times more grave according to the gravity of the law around which the dispensatory act revolves.

Article IV. The Actual Existence of the Cause

It has already been noted that while the Pope can dispense validly without a cause, in practice he never does but always insists on the presence of a true and just cause. It has been shown, too, that for the bishop to dispense validly from any general ecclesiastical law a just and reasonable cause must be present.[46] In this article the justice and reasonableness of the cause will be taken for granted and stress will be placed on the grave necessity of the cause alleged being truly existent. That it is of the utmost importance that the cause should really exist is clear if the notions concerning a dispensatory act are borne in mind.

In the first place it can be stated that the Pope never intends to dispense unless a just cause is present.[47] If the cause alleged for a

[44] *Cf.* Ep. encycl., *Satis Vobis,* 17 November, 1741, § 6—*Fontes,* n. 319.

[45] Canon 1104.

[46] Canon 84, § 1.

[47] *Cf.* Conc. Trid., sess. XXIV, *de ref. matr.*, c. 5; Benedictus XIV, *De Synodo Dioecesana,* XIII, c. 5, n. 7; S. C. de Prop. F., litt. encycl.. 11 Mart., 1868.

dispensation is not true it must of necessity be false and hence non-existent. But a false cause cannot be a just one. When therefore a dispensation from a matrimonial impediment is obtained by reason of a false cause the intention of the Pope to dispense is wanting entirely and the dispensation so obtained is invalid.[48]

When a minor impediment is involved, however, the falsification of the cause will not invalidate it, whether this falsification took place in good or bad faith. According to Canon 1042, § 1, there are five minor impediments, namely, consanguinity in the third degree of the collateral line, affinity in the second degree of the collateral line, public honesty in the second degree, spiritual relationship and crime arising from adultery with the promise or attempt of marriage even though only a civil act. In Canon 1054 it is stated that obreption or subreption will not render invalid a dispensation from a minor impediment even though the single final cause is false.

It should be borne in mind that a matrimonial impediment is a barrier placed by law which, if the impediment is diriment, renders the valid contracting of a marriage impossible.[49] By means of a valid dispensation this barrier or impediment is removed.[50] If, however, the dispensation is invalid the impediment has not been removed and the valid contracting of a marriage still remains an impossibility.

For a dispensation to be valid the one dispensing must have the power to dispense [51] and, if he is an inferior dispensing in the law of a superior, he must also have a just and reasonable cause on which to base his dispensatory act.[52] To grant a dispensation by reason of a false cause is equivalent to granting a dispensation without a cause, for the falsification of a cause implies that no cause really exists.[53]

[48] *Cf.* Giovine, *De Dispensationibus Matrimonialibus*, consult. IV, § LXIX, n. 1; Sanchez, *De Matrimonio*, L. VIII, disput. 17, n. 7: "Similiter non valet dispensatio inferioris in lege superioris, licet sit aliqualis causa, si tamen eam illegitimam esse constet. Quia idem est in hoc non esse causam et non esse justam."

[49] Canon 1036, § 2.

[50] Canon 80.

[51] *Cf.* Canon 80.

[52] *Cf.* Canon 84, § 1.

[53] *Cf.* Sanchez, *De Matrimonio*, L. VIII, disput. 17, n. 7.

The effect of a falsified cause on a dispensation is to be drawn from the prescriptions of Canon 40. In this canon it is stated that in all rescripts the condition is understood, even though not expressed: "Provided the petitions are founded on truth." Two exceptions to this general rule are provided for in this same canon, namely, in *Motu proprio* rescripts only the single final cause need be truthful [54] and again by force of Canon 1054 a dispensation conceded for a minor impediment is valid even though the final cause is false.

Ordinarily a matrimonial dispensation comes to the parties concerned through a rescript from the bishop. Hence when the bishop grants a dispensation he says in substance: "The impediment which impedes your marriage is removed provided your petition for the dispensation is founded on truth." Naturally one of the elements of truth is to be found in the truthfulness of the cause alleged. If the cause alleged is false, the fault of obreption, or the expression of a falsehood, is said to be present.[55] Bearing in mind that the concern here rests with the causes for matrimonial dispensations, obreption in the petitions for such dispensations will be the only consideration. There will be no need to consider the fault of subreption, or the deliberate concealment of the truth [56] for when a cause alleged for a major dispensation is false the dispensation is invalid not by reason of subreption but rather because of obreption.

In Canon 42, § 2, it is stated that the narration of a falsehood (obreption) in a rescript will not render the rescript invalid provided the final cause is true. This final cause can be the single cause proposed or if many equally weighty causes are alleged, only one need be true to make the rescript valid.[57] When only impelling causes are alleged, obreption found only in one cause can invalidate the rescript since all the impelling causes must simultaneously unite to form a motivating cause. Accordingly, the sole reason alleged, or the one motivating cause must be true.[58] This is the general principle, namely, that obreption will not vitiate a rescript provided the motivating

[54] Canon 42.
[55] Sipos, *Enchiridion Juris Canonici*, p. 34.
[56] *Cf.* Canon 42, § 1.
[57] *Cf.* Canon 42, § 2.
[58] *Cf.* Cicognani, *Commentarium ad Librum I Codicis*, p. 223.

cause is true. The exception to this principle is found in Canon 1054.[59]

An illustration will serve to explain better how the allegation of a false cause can invalidate the dispensation involved. Two persons between whom there exists the diriment impediment of disparity of cult, desire to contract marriage *coram ecclesia.* The parties present themselves to the proper pastor and reveal the existing impediment. From a cursory examination of the case the pastor can find no canonical cause on which to petition the dispensation and on his own volition he alleges as the cause, "*spes fundata conversionis partis acatholicae.*" The pastor knows full well, however, that the non-Catholic party has no intention whatever of converting and that his only interest in the Catholic Church rests in his willingness to acquiesce to the wishes of the Catholic party in her desire to marry before a priest. In the course of events the Ordinary grants the dispensation being prompted to do so on the final cause alleged, "*spes fundata conversionis partis acatholicae.*" In reality this cause never existed in the case in question. The cause alleged was false and the dispensation was fraudulently obtained since the prescription of Canon 40 was disregarded, namely, "*si preces veritate nitantur.*" Moreover, the impediment of disparity of cult was not removed by the dispensation fraudulently obtained so that the marriage taking place on the strength of the invalid dispensation was itself invalid and the invalidity of the marriage can be traced directly to the nonexistence of the cause alleged for the dispensation.[60] This case is illustrated simply to stress the fact that a cause must truly exist to make a dispensation granted by an inferior valid.[61] Unless the dispensation is valid the impediment remains in force. If the impediment is a diriment major impediment the marriage cannot be contracted validly since such an impediment, so long as it is in force, makes the valid contracting of marriage an impossibility.[62] If the impediment involved is an im-

[59] *Cf.* Canon 1042, § 2.

[60] *Cf. Thesaurus Resolutionum Sacrae Congregationis Concilii,* Tomus II, Allegata, p. 199 (a. 1721-1723): "Dispensatio fundata in falsa causa nulla est, licet falsitas processerit ex ignorantia."

[61] *Cf.* Canon 84, § 1.

[62] Canon 1036, § 2.

pedient impediment as, for example, mixed religion, the dispensation obtained without a cause really existing is certainly invalid, but the subsequent marriage is valid because a valid marriage can be contracted regardless of the presence of an impedient impediment.[63] From this it is not to be inferred, however, that the Ordinary can indiscriminately dispense from a minor impediment without a just cause. As a matter of fact the five minor impedments are diriment impediments and of themselves can form an invalidating barrier to any marriage. They are called *minor* probably because a dispensation from them can be obtained more easily.[64] But in dispensing from them the bishop must be governed by the principles surrounding dispensatory acts and as an inferior he can dispense validly only for a just cause. The redeeming feature extended in Canon 1054 lies in this, that after the bishop has granted a dispensation from a minor impediment the preliminary step has been taken to remove the impediment, namely the dispensatory act, and since the cause alleged was presumably true the impediment is removed. If later it is discovered that the final cause was false, the falsity (and hence the absence) of the cause will not result in the invalidity of the dispensation already obtained.[65]

While it is only in the case involving a major diriment impediment that the absence of a cause will work to the invalidity of the subsequent marriage, nevertheless the known absence of a cause in cases where impedient and minor diriment impediments are involved will cause the subsequent marriages in these cases to be illicit.[66] It is difficult to conceive that a bishop himself would be indifferent to the presence or absence of a cause. Through force of circumstances he must rely on the word of the pastor through whom the parties are petitioning dispensation that the cause alleged really exists. If the pastor is aware that no cause exists and deliberately supplies one for the convenience of the case he is guilty of fraud and can be punished

[63] Canon 1036, § 1.

[64] *Cf.* Ayrinhac-Lydon, *Marriage Legislation in the New Code of Canon Law*, n. 87.

[65] *Cf.* Vermeersch-Creusen, *Epitome Juris Canonici,* II, n. 318.

[66] *Cf.* Ayrinhac-Lydon, *Marriage Legislation in the New Code of Canon Law*, n. 87.

by the Ordinary according to the gravity of his guilt.[67] The pastor has no right whatever to insert a cause deliberately in the petition for a matrimonial dispensation when he knows in reality that the cause alleged does not exist. By his negligence and temerity he is responsible for the invalid dispensatory act of the bishop and the invalidity of the subsequent marriage, provided the impediment involved is a major diriment impediment, can be placed directly on the conscience of the pastor who has presumed to supply the cause.

Artice V. The Examination of the Existing Cause

The Council of Trent [68] and many of the Decretists and Decretalists[69] required that the actual existence of the cause be known to the one dispensing. In the strict analysis of this prescription the one dispensing could not validly dispense when he knew of the existence of the cause only on the word of another. He himself would have to know, on his own examination, that the cause on which the dispensation was being petitioned actually existed.[70] But it is agreed that the examination or knowledge of the cause is required rather for the liceity than for the validity of a dispensation granted by a superior.[71] Concerning the validity in the granting of a dispensation a few distinctions must be made.

It is commonly admitted that, without an examination of the cause, the legislator can dispense validly from his own laws, from the laws of his predecessor and from the laws of his inferior.[72] This would logically follow from the principle that the legislator can dispense validly in the aforementioned instances even without a cause.[73] If he can dispense validly without a cause, surely he can dispense validly without examining the existence of the cause.

[67] *Cf.* Canon 2361.

[68] Conc. Trid., sess. XXV, *de ref.*, c. 18.

[69] *Cf.* Brys, *De Dispensatione in Jure Canonico*, pp. 193-195.

[70] In fact Innocent IV advocated the institution of at least a summary process that the one dispensing might determine the existence of the cause alleged. *Cf.* Brys, *De Dispensatione in Jure Canonico*, p. 193.

[71] *Cf.* Wernz, *Jus Decretalium*, I, n. 124; Maroto, *Institutiones Juris Canonici*, n. 306; A Coronata, *Institutiones Juris Canonici*, I, n. 115.

[72] *Cf.* Michiels, *Normae Generales*, II, p. 508.

[73] *Cf.* Cicognani, *Commentarium ad Librum I Codicis*, p. 333.

If it is a question of a dispensation granted by an inferior who has not examined the cause a further distinction must be noted. When an inferior, acting through delegated power, fails to examine the cause and *de facto* the cause is lacking, then the dispensation is invalid. But in this instance the invalidity does not arise from the failure of the one dispensating to examine the existence of the cause but rather from the objective non-existence of the cause required for a valid dispensation when an inferior dispenses.[74]

It is not necessary, however, that the inferior should personally ascertain the presence of the cause but he should be sure that the one who alleges the cause, whether he be the petitioner himself, or the pastor, for instance, of the petitioner, can be believed. Whatever investigation may be necessary can be delegated. Under the present discipline, however, it will be rare when the invalidity of a matrimonial dispensation will arise from the failure of the one dispensing to examine the existence of the cause. In Canon 40 it is stated that in all rescripts there is to be understood the condition, even though not expressed, *"si preces veritate nitantur."* By these words it is implied that, objectively, it is necessary only that the cause on which the petition is based is actually true. Before 1885 the phrase commonly inserted in rescripts was worded: *"si preces veritate niti repereris."* [75] It is not difficult to conclude that this phrase places on the one dispensing the obligation of actually (not personally) determining the existence of the cause. Hence if the one who grants the dispensation acts contrary to the condition placed by the superior his dispensatory act will be invalid regardless of the objective existence of the cause.[76]

If the validity of the dispensation does not depend on the grantor's knowledge of the actual existence of the cause, the dispensation will be valid provided the cause actually exists although unknown to the one dispensing because the value of a dispensation depends not on the cognition of the cause but on its actual existence.[77]

The foregoing principles can have their practical application in

[74] *Cf.* Michiels, *Normae Generales,* II, p. 508.

[75] *Cf.* O'Neill, *Papal Rescripts of Favor,* p. 117.

[76] *Cf.*. Sanchez, *De Matrimonio,* L. VIII, disput. 34, n. 25.

[77] *Cf.* Sanchez, *De Matrimonio,* L. VIII, disput. 17, n. 11.

certain instances. A few of the more common cases will be noted:

1. When it is certainly known that a just cause for dispensing is present the one dispensing acts validly and licitly. Moreover, when the dispensation has been obtained the petitioner may validly and licitly take advantage of the favor granted. These deductions are but the simple application of Canon 84, § 1, which states that dispensation from an ecclesiastical law can be granted only when a just and reasonable cause is present; otherwise a dispensation granted without cause by an inferior will be both invalid and illicit.[78]

2. When it is certainly known (bad faith being present) that a just cause for dispensing is lacking, the dispensatory act of an inferior will be both invalid and illicit [79] except in those cases in which the dispensation involved concerns matrimonial impediments of a minor grade.[80] Moreover, the petitioner who is a party to this fraud can neither validly nor licitly take advantage of the favor granted by the inferior who knows that a just cause does not exist. This is simply a natural deduction because the petitioner cannot make use of a favor that does not exist and an inferior cannot bring a favor into existence except for a just cause.[81]

If, on the contrary, the petitioner, knowing that the cause is lacking, asks for a dispensation from the legislator himself, and the legislator, knowing that a cause does not exist, grants the dispensation, his dispensatory act is valid, although illicit. In such an instance, if scandal is excluded, the petitioner can validly and licitly use the favor granted. This conclusion rests on the principle that the legislator can dispense validly without a cause. In so dispensing the obligatory force of the law is taken away, even though illicitly. Hence the petitioner is no longer bound by the law and can validly and licitly use the favor granted. Moreover the petitioner does not cooperate in the illicit act of the legislator because he simply makes use of the effect coming from the dispensatory act of the legislator and there is no malice in this effect.[82]

[78] *Cf.* Michiels, *Normae Generales*, II, p. 509.

[79] Canon 84, § 1.

[80] Canon 1054.

[81] Canon 84, § 1.

[82] *Cf.* Suarez, *Tractatus de Legibus*, L. VI, c. 19, n. 14.

More frequently matrimonial dispensations are conceded by the bishop through delegated power. Hence the bad faith of the petitioners will beget an invalid dispensation. It is difficult to conceive of a bishop deliberately granting a matrimonial dispensation when he knows that a just cause is lacking. But it is entirely possible and probable that a person who is bound by a matrimonial impediment will ask for a dispensation when he is aware that the necessary cause is not present. The bad faith of the petitioner will nullify the dispensatory act of the bishop since in such cases the bishop grants dispensation on the condition, *"si preces veritate nitantur."* [83]

3. When erroneously, in good faith, it is thought that a just cause for dispensing is present, but *de facto* this cause is lacking:

The one dispensing does not sin and neither does the one seeking the dispensation sin in petitioning it.[84] When, however, the error is discovered a distinction must be made. If the dispensation is granted by the legislator it is certainly valid because he who dispenses from his own law even without a cause, dispenses validly.[85] Or if the dispensation involved concerns an impediment of minor grade,[86] it will be valid regardless of the lack of cause.

If, however, the dispensation has been granted by an inferior through power conceded to him, some authors,[87] hold that the dispensation becomes invalid as soon as the lack of cause is discovered. To say the least this opinion is in strict conformity with Canon 84, § 1, which states that for an inferior to dispense validly and licitly a just cause must be present. Michiels,[88] holds that on the presumed will of the superior the subsequent discovery of the absence of a cause should not render the dispensation invalid when the dispensation was sought and granted in good faith. Perhaps this opinion of Michiels should not be attacked directly but surely he is in error in quoting the authors who he claims give credence to his

[83] *Cf.* Canon 40. *Cf.* also O'Neill, *Papal Rescripts of Favor,* p. 117.

[84] *Cf.* Michiels, *Normae Generales,* II, p. 510.

[85] *Cf.* Cicognani, *Commentarium ad Librum I Codicis,* p. 333.

[86] *Cf.* Canon 1042, § 2.

[87] D'Annibale, *Summula Theologiae Moralis,* I, n. 233; Vermeersch-Creusen, *Epitome Juris Canonici,* I, n. 197; Raus, *Institutiones Canonicae,* n. 41.

[88] *Cf.* Michiels, *Normae Generales,* II, p. 510.

statements. He would have Sanchez and Schmalzgruber claim that if in good faith a dispensation is sought and granted on the strength of a cause which erroneously is thought to exist, the dispensation continues valid after it is discovered that the cause never existed. In reality both these authors are considering a case in which a sufficient cause is present but which subsequently is discovered to be insufficient. This subsequent insufficiency of a cause is something quite different than the subsequent discovery of the nonexistence of a cause for in the first instance a cause was really present and hence there is something on which to base the dispensation; in the latter instance no cause ever existed.

Sanchez [89] states his theory in the words: "Similiter non valet dispensatio inferioris in lege superioris, *licet sit aliqualis causa,* si tamen eam illegitimam esse constet. Quia idem est in hoc non esse causam et non esse justam. Atque ita doctores asserunt eam dispensationem absque causa legitima et justa esse irritam. Hoc tamen limitarem, nisi prudenter, ac bona fide judicarit praelatus causam esse justam. Tunc enim credo valere dispensationem, *licet non fuit causa sufficiens.* Quia non est credendum aliam esse Pontificis intentionem circa suas leges et Dei circa suas, in quibus permittitur inferiori dispensare."

The case as Schmalzgrueber [90] treats it reads: "An valida dispensatio facta *ex causa* quam orator fideliter exposuit, et dispensans bona fide, et rationabiliter putavit esse justam, et sufficientem, licet revera esset *insufficiens.*" This author solves the question in the same way in which Sanchez does, namely, when a just cause that is present is considered, in good faith, to be sufficient and subsequently is discovered to have been insufficient, the dispensation granted on the strength of the insufficient cause can be held as probably valid from the presumed will of the superior. Hence it would seem that Michiels has erred in his interpretation of Sanchez and Schmalzgrueber and he further adds to his error in applying the prescriptions of Canon 6, n. 2, to his erroneous interpretation of these authors. It is the claim of Michiels that Canon 84, § 1, institutes no new legis-

[89] Sanchez, *De Matrimonio,* L. VIII, disput. 17, n. 7, 8.

[90] Schmalzgrueber, *Jus Ecclesiasticum,* L. IV, t. 16, n. 166.

lation on the doctrine of dispensation but takes the doctrine over *ex integro* from the ancient discipline. Therefore, he argues, the opinion of those ancient authors, namely Sanchez and Schmalzgrueber, should be accepted. This reasoning of Michiels would be in perfect accord with the application of Canon 6, n. 2, if it were not for the fact that Sanchez and Schmalzgrueber were speaking of the subsequent discovery of the insufficiency of some cause and not the subsequent discovery of the nonexistence of a cause which originally was thought to have been present.

By the terms of Canon 84, § 1, when the nonexistence of a cause is discovered the dispensation, though sought and granted in good faith, must be considered invalid. In actual practice, however, some solution to such a case should be found. If the principles of Canon 84, § 1, were imposed on every such case grave inconvenience and harm could result in the forced dissolution of the common life in instances where the parties have lived in the married state for an extended period and perhaps have children. If such parties were told that no marriage bond ever existed between them and that it would be necessary for them to separate, aside from causing grave inconvenience such a course would occasion grave scandal among those who naturally believed that the parties involved were validly married. In such an instance the more prudent procedure would be the application of a *sanatio in radice* or if the parties themselves can be approached a new dispensation may be issued and a simple convalidation can follow. In those cases, however, where the parties are not living together and have obtained a civil divorce the principles of Canon 84, § 1, could be invoked to support the nullity of the marriage contracted on the strength of a dispensation which in reality never existed because of the nonexistence of a cause.

Aside from the apparent misinterpretation which Michiels places on the case treated by Sanchez and Schmalzgrueber, it is difficult to find any intrinsic value in the opinion he advances whereby a dispensation subsequently discovered to be null because of the nonexistence of a cause should be considered as valid from the interpreted will of the superior. It is hardly probable that a marriage contracted in such circumstances would ever be held as valid if its validity were attacked in an ecclesiastical court.

4. When, erroneously, in good faith, it is thought that a just cause for dispensing is not present when *de facto* it does exist:

The dispensatory act of the one dispensing and the use of the dispensation by the petitioner will be *illicit* since each one has the deliberate intention to place an action which they believe is contrary to the law.[91] Nevertheless the dispensation is undoubtedly valid because *de facto* the cause exists and the value of a dispensation is taken from the actual existence of the necessary cause.[92]

5. When there is a doubt concerning the existence of a just cause:

In order to propose a solution to this supposition it will be well to consider the second paragraph of Canon 84:

"Dispensatio in dubio de sufficientia causae licite petitur et potest licite et valide concedi."

In the strict sense this canon contains the governing norm for dispensatory acts when a doubt arises, not concerning the existence of a cause, but rather concerning the sufficiency of a cause which is known already to exist.[93] In such circumstances the petitioner may licitly ask for a dispensation, advancing as a reason the doubtfully sufficient cause, and the one dispensing can rest his dispensatory act on that cause and may licitly and validly grant the dispensation.[94] It is generally agreed among the authors that any cause probably just will suffice for a licit and valid dispensation.[95] The Church is liberal on this point that anxieties and scruples may not be aroused. Moreover, the dispensation granted for a probably just cause will remain valid even if afterward it is discovered that the cause was less just than originally supposed.[96]

[91] Canon 84, § 1.

[92] *Cf.* Sanchez, *De Matrimonio,* L. VII, disput. 17, n. 11; Michiels, *Normae Generales,* II, p. 511.

[93] *Cf.* Vermeersch-Creusen, *Epitome Juris Canonici,* I, n. 197; A. Coronata, *Institutiones Juris Canonici,* 1, n. 115.

[94] *Cf.* Canon 84, § 2; Vermeersch-Creusen, *Epitome Juris Canonici,* I, n. 197; Cicognani, *Commentarium ad Librum I Codicis,* p. 334.

[95] *Cf.* A. Coronata, *Institutiones Juris Canonici,* I, n. 115.

[96] D'Annibale, *Summula Theologiae Moralis,* I, 233, note 27 and 31; A. Coronata, *Institutiones Juris Canonici,* I, n. 115; Michiels, *Normae Generales,* II, p. 511; Chelodi, *Jus de Personis,* n. 88.

If the Code permits the valid and licit granting of a dispensation when there is doubt concerning the sufficiency of the cause, what is to be done in practice if the doubt concerns the very existence of the cause? It would seem that Canon 84, § 2, could not be extended to include this case for the canon speaks specifically of the doubtful sufficiency of the cause. On the contrary, some authors [97] hold that Canon 84, § 2, can be extended because there seems to be no real difference between a doubt concerning the sufficiency of a cause and a doubt concerning the existence of a just cause. But there is a difference because in the one case, namely when there is a doubt concerning the sufficiency of the cause, Canon 84, § 2, allows the one dispensing to raise the doubtfully sufficient cause to the status and strength of a really sufficient cause and the validity of this cause cannot afterward be questioned. In the other instance it is doubted whether or not the cause exists. Hence a cause which really exists at the time when the dispensation is granted, but concerning the sufficiency of which there is question, surely differs from a cause which questionably exists or does not exist at all at the time when the dispensation is granted. Canon 84, § 2, will supply the sufficiency wanting in a doubtfully sufficient cause that subsequently scruples may not arise. When there is a doubt concerning the existence of the cause Canon 84, § 1, must be invoked for a cause either exists or does not exist. If it exists and is just and grave in proportion to the law from which dispensation is being sought, the dispensation can be validly and licitly granted even by an inferior in the law of a superior. If the doubt concerning the existence of the cause cannot be resolved the inferior is powerless to dispense since no canon can be invoked whereby he can dispense without a cause or raise a doubtfully existing cause to the status of a sufficient cause.

Article VI. The Effect of the Cessation of the Cause Upon the Dispensation

According to Canon 86, a dispensation which has a *tractus successivus* ceases in the same way as does a privilege and also by the

[97] D'Annibale, *Summula Theologiae Moralis,* I, n. 233, notes 27 and 31; A. Coronata, *Institutiones Juris Canonici,* I, n. 115, ad 1.

total cessation of the final cause. A dispensation is said to possess a *tractus successivus* when it regards many successive acts as for instance a dispensation from the law of fasting.[98] There is no difficulty in understanding that when the final cause ceases for a dispensation having a *tractus successivus* the dispensation itself will cease. It will not be denied that when a dispensation from the law of fasting is granted because of the physical debility of the petitioner, the dispensation will become ineffective as soon as the petitioner is restored to health.

On the contrary, however, a matrimonial dispensation has no *tractus successivus* since the effect for which the dispensation is intended, namely, the removal of the impediment, is accomplished by a single act.[99]

The only concern here is with matrimonial dispensations and since such a dispensation is single and has no *tractus successivus* the prescriptions of Canon 86 will be of little aid in determining whether a matrimonial dispensation becomes void if the final cause ceases between the time of the granting of the dispensation and the celebration of the marriage.

It is not claiming too much in saying that post-Code authors together with several of the older authors are practically unanimous.[100] in holding that a dispensation accomplished through a single dispensatory act, as, for instance, a matrimonial dispensation, does not cease if the final cause should cease after the dispensation has been granted. In virtue of this opinion a matrimonial dispensation obtained for the cause *legitimatio prolis* will not become void if

[98] *Cf.* Michiels, *Normae Generales,* II, pp. 461, 462; Cocchi, *Commentarium in Codicem Juris Canonici,* I, p. 297; Cicognani, *Commentarium ad Librum I Codicis,* p. 318.

[99] *Cf.* Maroto, *Institutiones Juris Canonici,* n. 303; Michiels, *Normae Generales,* II, p. 461.

[100] Chelodi, *Jus de Personis,* n. 88; À Coronata, *Institutiones Juris Canonici,* I, n. 117, ad 1; Cocchi, *Commentarium in Codicem Juris Canonici,* I, p. 298; Michiels, *Normae Generales,* II, p. 523; Cicognani, *Commentarium ad Librum I Codicis,* p. 336; Maroto, *Institutiones Juris Canonici,* n. 309c; Noldin, I, *De Principiis,* n. 188; Schmalzgrueber, *Jus Ecclesiasticum Universum,* IX, tract. 16, n. 163; Suarez, *Tractatus De Legibus,* L. VI, c. 20, n. 15; De Justis, *De Dispensationibus Matrimonialibus,* L. III, c. 1, n. 2.

the child happens to die during the time elapsing between the granting of the dispensation and the celebration of the marriage.[101] The reasons on which the authors base their opinion in holding to the continued validity of a single dispensation notwithstanding the cessation of the final cause are clearly logical. In the first place, through a dispensation the impediment impeding the marriage has been removed. This is the total effect of the dispensatory act. When an impediment is removed it does not again revive except through an act of the superior,[102] because only the supreme authority in the Church has the right to establish impediments.[103] In short, when the one dispensing through delegated power grants the dispensation his power becomes exhausted.[104] When the effect of the dispensation has been obtained, namely, the removal of the impediment, the dispensatory act will have no further bearing on the future marriage. It is of no consequence, then, that the final cause might cease between the granting of the dispensation and the celebration of the marriage. It is sufficient that the final cause remained in existence until the dispensation itself was granted for the cause was the *reason* for the dispensation.[105]

The second reason advanced in support of this opinion lies in the fact that in the old law as well as in the legislation of the Code[106] the condition on which rescripts are granted is understood to be: *"si ita est"* or *"si preces veritate nitantur."*

Such expressions can only mean that the petitions imploring the dispensation are true when the dispensation is granted. If the validity of the dispensation itself were to remain uncertain until the time

[101] *Cf.* Cocchi, *Commentarium in Codicem Juris Canonici,* I, p. 288. But in such an instance the dispensation could become void if, for example, the father of the child was bound by a vow; but only if it was definitely stated that he was dispensed from the vow for the purpose of contracting *this* particular marriage and for *this* particular reason, namely, *legitimatio prolis.*

[102] *Cf.* Suarez, *Tractatus De Legibus,* L. VI, c. 20, n. 15; c. 9, X, *de filiis presbyterorum ordinandis vel non,* I, 17.

[103] *Cf.* Canon 1038, § 2.

[104] *Cf.* Sanchez, *De Matrimonio,* L. VIII, disput. 27, n. 39.

[105] *Cf.* Giovine, *De Dispensationibus Matrimonialibus,* I, consult. IV, § LXXV, n. 4.

[106] *Cf.* Canon 40.

when it is used, the clause *"dummodo causa perseveret"* would have to be inserted. When, therefore, such a clause is not inserted, the dispensation will be valid, *"si preces veritate nitantur,"* at the time when the dispensation is granted and the cause need not further persevere beyond that time.[108]

[107] *Cf.* Schmalzgrueber, *Jus Ecclesiasticum Universum,* IX, tract. 16, n. 163; Giovine, *De Dispensationibus Matrimonialibus,* I consult. IV, § LXXV, n. 4.

CHAPTER VII

THE CANONICAL CAUSES PROPOSED BY THE SACRED CONGREGATION OF THE PROPAGATION OF THE FAITH

ARTICLE I. THE INSTRUCTION OF THE PROPAGANDA, MAY 9, 1877

ON May 9, 1877, the Sacred Congregation for the Propagation of the Faith saw fit to issue an instruction on the causes for matrimonial dispensations.[1] This instruction is a significant document. In a few brief words the Congregation has given a summary of the principle of dispensation from matrimonial impediment together with an enumeration of some of the causes requisite and sufficient for such an act.

The opening sentence of the Instruction embodies the notions of dispensation as advanced by the canonists since the eleventh century. To this end the Instruction opens with the words: "Since dispensation is the relaxation of the common law made with a knowledge of the cause by him who has the power, it is clear to all that dispensations from matrimonial impediments are not to be conceded, unless a legitimate and grave cause should intervene." As has been said, no new principle is enunciated here. The Congregation is simply stressing the importance and necessity of a just and grave cause for dispensation and particularly for a dispensation from matrimonial impediments. Since matrimony is a public act, it is of the utmost importance that dispensation from the impediments established in regard to marriage, should conform strictly to the canonical principles of the act of dispensing. If a strict vigilance is not enforced on this phase of dispensatory acts untold harm can be wrought. Hence the insistence by the Propaganda that matrimonial impediments are not to be dispensed from except for a legitimate and grave cause. In determining in general the quality of the cause the Instruction continues: "Indeed, it is easily understood that the gravity of

[1] S. C. P. F., 9 May, 1877—*Collect. P. F.*, n. 1470.

the cause will be in accordance with the gravity of the impediment which opposes the celebration of marriage." These words simply form a logical deduction. Prudence dictates that a greater reason should be advanced for dispensing, for example, from the diriment impediment of disparity of cult than from the diriment impediment of spiritual relationship. It is true that both are impediments placed by ecclesiastical law, that is, prescinding from the danger of perversion present in a disparate marriage, which makes disparity of cult an impediment according to the dictates of the divine law,[2] but the two impediments considered in themselves, are of unequal weight.

The failure and carelessness of petitioners seeking dispensation to advance worthy canonical causes in their petitions prompted the Holy See to take steps to avoid the spread of such abuses. Accordingly an Instruction concerning canonical causes was published. To quote the Instruction: "It is by no means rare that suppliant letters come to the Holy See seeking some dispensations of this kind which are supported by no canonical reason. It sometimes happens also that in supplications of this nature those things are omitted, which necessarily should be expressed, lest the dispensation suffer from nullity." To avoid this fault the Holy See thought it of timely importance to suggest, through the Propaganda, some causes, which according to the *stylus curiae* and approbation of the Holy See, are canonical causes for matrimonial dispensations. Further, the purpose of the Instruction was to indicate those things which ought to be expressed in petitioning for dispensation. This intention is expressed by the Congregation in the words: "It therefore seems opportune in the present Instruction, to enumerate briefly the principal causes which are accustomed to be regarded as sufficient for obtaining matrimonial dispensations according to the canonical sanctions and prudent judgment of ecclesiastical provision." This sentence is of significant interest in treating of canonical causes. It will be noted that the Congregation remarks that the principal canonical causes will be listed. This definitely confirms the notion of the list as being compiled *demonstrative* and not *taxative* and hence admits the possibility of other just and grave causes. It would seem that the Holy See acts prudently in not listing, *taxative,* causes for matrimonial

[2] Canon 1060.

dispensations for very frequently the circumstances surrounding various marriages cases are so involved and utterly different that perhaps causes listed *taxative* could not possibly be applied to the cases in question.[3] Furthermore it is commonly accepted that the one dispensing is to judge the sufficiency of the cause alleged,[4] and that he is to be guided by the existing curial practice.[5] But this demonstrative list of causes compiled by the Propaganda is valuable since it definitely fixes the causes enumerated as being of sufficient weight, *servatis servandis,* for moving the Holy See to concede the dispensation sought. In short, the list affords a guiding norm also for dispensatory acts based on other grave and just causes.

The preface of the Instruction concludes with the words: "In this regard it will be of value to observe that sometimes a single cause taken separately will be insufficient, but if joined to another will be sufficient according to the axiom: things which singly naught avail, all together may prevail. From this statement it can be inferred that while the causes listed by the Propaganda are all canonical, they however, must be regarded, according to circumstances, as being either motivating or impulsive. The practice of considering all canonical causes of being of equal weight would seem as imprudent as attempting to enumerate *taxative* the causes themselves. Prudence dictates that cases for matrimonial dispensation must be examined individually. Furthermore it seems that an analogy can be drawn between this practice and the principles of dispensation as found in the Code. The definition declares that dispensation is the relaxing of a law in a particular case.[6] The particular case, therefore, is drawn from the many instances which are governed by the law and a special scrutiny is given this case. And again the

[3] In speaking of causes sufficient for dispensing from the impediment of mixed religion Gasparri, *De Matrimonio,* n. 448, remarks: "If you ask what might be a just, grave, legitimate, sufficient cause for which this dispensation is conceded, *per se* it is clear that a response absolutely certain in the abstract cannot be given since the circumstances of each case are always to be considered." If this is true in dispensation from the impediment of mixed religion, *a pari* it is true for any dispensation.

[4] Noldin, *De Principiis,* I, n. 186.

[5] Wernz, *Jus Decretalium,* I, n. 629, note 148.

[6] Canon 80.

Code[7] decrees that the justice of the cause be in direct proportion to the gravity of the law from which dispensation is sought. Hence that justice might be done, the circumstances surrounding each case should be weighed and the result should be arraigned against the law which is to be suspended. In a given case the circumstances might be of such proportions that a single canonical cause may become the single motivating cause for granting the dispensation. Or again the circumstances may be of so slight importance that several impulsive causes will have to be cumulatively invoked before one motivating cause can be found.

It is to be borne in mind that only the principal causes admitted by the Holy See for matrimonial dispensations are contained in this Instruction of the Propaganda. In reality the circumstances surrounding a particular case will determine the value of the cause on which the interested parties wish to base their petition for dispensation. Hence if the circumstances warrant it, the one dispensing may grant the dispensation for a cause not found among the causes enumerated by the Propaganda.

Article II. The Requisites for and Application of the Causes

1. Narrowness of Place (Angustia Loci)

Regularly this cause is granted only in favor of the woman. It exists, either absolutely or relatively, when, in the place of birth or even of domicile, the relationship of the woman is very extensive. Because of this fact she is unable to find, except among her relatives a man equal to her in social standing whom she might marry. Furthermore she would find it difficult to leave the place for a more populous center where her choice of a husband would be broadened.[8]

Such is the first cause listed by the Propaganda. In the first place a commentary will be made on the wording of the cause and later an estimate of the practical value and application of the cause will be set forth.

[7] Canon 84, § 1.

[8] *Cf.* S. C. P. F., Instruction, 9 May, 1877, n. 1—*Collect. P. F.*, n. 1470.

In order that the cause of *angustia loci* may be advanced for seeking a dispensation two conditions must be verified, namely, in the place in which the woman lives she is unable to find a husband except among her relatives, who is of equal standing with her in the community, and secondly, she would find it difficult to establish a residence in a more populated place where she would be more likely to find a greater number of eligible men from whom to choose a husband.

From the exact wording of the Instruction the cause of *angustia loci* is to be advanced only when petitioning dispensation from the impediments of consanguinity and affinity. More will be said about this later.

By the word "place" as used in the Instruction is understood any assemblage of dwellings, as a city, a town, a canton, a village, which is distinct, either by reason of name or government, or by reason of distance. For instance, a village which is removed a mile in distance from another community is said to be distinct in itself.[9]

A place can be small taken either absolutely or relatively. Absolute *angustia loci* is determined from the nature of the place taken in itself. If the town does not contain more than three hundred homes or fifteen hundred inhabitants, regardless of age or sex, it is absolutely small.[10] In computing the number of homes and inhabitants, infidels, heretics and schismatics probably are excluded but not impious or indifferent Catholics.[11]

A town is relatively small if, regardless of the fact that it contains more than three hundred homes or fifteen hundred inhabitants, a woman, because of her position, cannot find a marriageable equal.[12] It is not sufficient to visualize the possibility of relative *angustia loci*. It could so happen that a few Catholics belonging to a particular for-

[9] *Cf.* Vromant, *Jus Missionariorum,* V; *De Matrimonio,* n. 144.

[10] Gasparri, *De Matrimonio,* n. 303, note 1; Prümmer, *Manuale Theologiae Moralis,* III, n. 862.

[11] *Cf.* Vlaming, *Praelectiones Juris Matrimonii,* II, n. 423;—Vromant, *Jus Missionariorum,* V; *De Matrimonio,* n. 144. Those places exceeding three hundred families or fifteen hundred inhabitants cannot claim absolute *angustia.* This has been expressly declared by Pius IX in a letter per Card. Pro Datarium datis 30 August, 1847, apud Giovine, t. 1, p. 373 et t. 2, p. 207 (ubi assignat diem 6 September), Feije, *De Imped.,* n. 652, p. 610.

[12] Cappello, *De Sacramentis,* III, n. 260.

eign nation are living in a populated city. A certain woman, desirous of contracting marriage, may be related to almost every acceptable suitor in this national group. She may not be able to marry, or desirous of marrying, any Catholic man who is ignorant of her native tongue and customs. Hence for her the only satisfactory marriage could be contracted among her relatives and countrymen. In this instance the city taken in itself is not small since its population exceeds the prescribed number of inhabitants, but considering the particular case of such a woman, the city, relatively taken, is small.

Furthermore the place advanced as the reason for dispensation may be either the woman's birthplace or domicile. *A fortiori,* if both these places are small the cause can be admitted and then a state of *angustia locorum* would exist.[13] Here it can be asked if the cause can be extended to the smallness of the quasi-domicile? A quasi-domicile is obtained by living in a place with the intention of remaining there the greater part of the year or by residence protracted beyond the greater part of the year.[14] The small size of the quasi-domicile cannot be invoked as a cause if the woman has some other domicile in which she lives; but if she has no other domicile, or having one, does not live in it, the small size of the quasi-domicile can be advanced as a cause.[15] Likewise if a woman has two domiciles and only one of them is small she cannot plead *angustia loci* because the larger domicile will offset the smaller one.[16]

In the place, either absolutely or relatively small, the relatives of the woman must be so numerous that she finds it impossible to choose a worthy husband except among her own kindred or affines. The worthiness and equality of the prospective husband need be taken only in a wide sense. If the woman herself comes from an honest and upright family and is herself beyond moral reproach,[17] she can claim inequality of station if any of the men whom she would be forced to marry, were she to seek outside her family, are old while

[13] Gasparri, *De Matrimonio,* n. 303, note 1.

[14] Canon 92, § 2.

[15] Feije, *De Impedimentis,* p. 609, n. 651.

[16] Gasparri, *De Matrimonio,* n. 303, note 1.

[17] Cappello, *De Sacramentis,* III, n. 260f; Feije, *De Impedimentis,* p. 611, n. 653.

she herself is young; or are poor while she is rich; or are uneducated or of questionable morals and religious habits.[18] All these conditions would constitute an unequal marriage and this is the danger the Church has always been desirous of averting.[19]

If these are the types of men who live in the town and are unrelated to her, the woman can plead that, except within her own family, she is unable to find a worthy equal whom she might marry. The Church is very liberal in the interpretation she places on the woman's inability to find a suitable husband.

It is sufficient that at the time when the dispensation is sought, no worthy man living in the place is seeking the woman's hand in marriage or that such a condition in the near future is probable.[20] The fact that a suitable man or men may have sought the woman in marriage at some prior time need not be considered. For the present she is without a worthy suitor and this is the condition admitted in the cause. Even if she has refused prior proposals of marriage with the express intention of afterward seeking dispensation by reason of narrowness of place, the woman would be acting within her rights and if such a dispensation were granted it would be valid even if the mention of such a premeditated purpose were not made.[21] Furthermore, if there happen to be two or three men[22] living in the town who are willing and eligible to marry the woman, she can still seek dispensation by reason of narrowness of place, because it is proper that in choosing a partner for marriage a person's choice should not be confined to such a narrow range.[23] Nor is it necessary to make a minute search of the town for a suitable husband before the woman can petition dispensation on the plea of narrowness of place. In the opinion of St. Ambrose it is unbecoming womanly modesty for a woman to seek a husband.[24] Hence to take advantage

[18] Payen, *De Matrimonio,* I, n. 740.

[19] *Cf.* Sanchez *De Matrimoni,* L. VIII, disput. 1, n. 15.

[20] De Justis, *De Dispensationibus Matrimonialibus,* L. III, c. 2.

[21] Gasparri, *De Matrimonio,* n. 303, note 1; Cappello, *De Sacramentis,* III, n. 260f.

[22] Dubia resolved 8 July, 1886—S. C. Conc.—*A. S. S.,* IX, p. 574.

[23] Gasparri, *De Matrimonio,* n. 303, note 1; Cappello, *De Sacramentis,* III, n. 260f; Sanchez, *De Matrimonio,* L. VIII, disput. 19, n. 14.

[24] C. 13, C. XXXII, q. 2.

of the law of dispensation on the grounds of *angustia loci* it suffices that, for a reasonable length of time, it has been known that the woman is desirous of marrying yet no eligible man has sought her. If then her hand has not been asked for in marriage it can reasonably be supposed that it will be difficult for her to find an equal who is not a relative.[25]

Another condition for the cause of *angustia loci* has been placed by the Propaganda. Besides being unable to find unrelated suitors in her community the woman must find it difficult and disagreeable to break her home ties and go to a more populated community where she would be liable to find a greater number of men from which to choose a suitable husband. If the woman would never find it painful to break home ties and if at the same time by so acting she could find an unrelated and suitable man who would seek her in marriage the cause of *angustia loci* could not properly be advanced. A similar condition is had when a woman, advancing the cause of *angustia loci,* asks permission to contract marriage with a relative who lives outside her own proper home and who intends to return to his own home as soon as the marriage takes place.[26] In either case, namely, when the woman experiences no difficulty in leaving home or if she were permitted to marry a relative away from her home, one of the principal reasons for the admission of the cause would be defeated for the Church permits the cause of *angustia loci* that the woman may not be forced to break home ties.[27] It would seem that in each instance the case should be examined to determine whether or not the woman would experience inconvenience in leaving home. In some cases a strict fulfillment of this cause could be demanded. In others the improper fulfillment of this and other conditions does not imply that the cause of *angustia loci* is vainly petitioned. There would always be possibility for it but in such incomplete instances the smallness of place cannot be alleged simply and without quaification. The circumstances surrounding the case should be explained, for instance that the place has more than fifteen hundred inhabitants but that the woman, because of her family position, is limited in the

[25] De Justis, *De Dispensationibus Matrimonialibus,* L. III, c. 2, n. 24.
[26] Vlaming, *Praelectiones Juris Matrimonii,* II, n. 423b.
[27] *Cf.* De Smet, *Betrothment and Marriage,* II, n. 817.

choice of a husband from the suitable men living in the town.[28] So also it can be stated that the prospective husband belongs to another place and intends to stay there.[29]

By the words of the Instruction, the cause of *angustia loci* can be invoked regularly only in favor of the woman.[30] This is as it should be for ordinarily the man will find little difficulty in seeking a suitable spouse. By nature it is less difficult for him to sever home ties and leave his native place if he finds that the proper selection of a wife is confined within too narrow bounds.[31] It is not impossible, however, that the cause of *angustia loci* can be verified for the man. The place in which the man lives may be so far distant from any other place, that if he should seek a wife outside his home he would be unable to induce her to live in the isolated community in which he makes his home.[32] The man would find it particularly difficult to persuade a woman to accompany him to his community if, besides its isolation, it was known for its poverty and for the hardships its inhabitants were forced to endure for obtaining a scant existence. In such instances the man would be forced either to remain unmarried or marry a woman inferior to him if, economically, such a state of affairs could be imagined when considering his dire poverty. But a man in the direst poverty could possibly marry beneath him by taking for a wife a woman of questionable morals.

De Smet seems to be about the only author who holds to the strict signification of the term "ratione tantum oratricis."[33] Without hesitation he claims that a man cannot invoke the cause of *angustia loci.* Such being his viewpoint, he logically concludes that when a Catholic man requires dispensation in order to marry a non-Catholic woman, *angustia loci* cannot be advanced, because, since the dispensation in such a case would directly affect the man, this cause would then be invoked in his favor.

It seems equitable to permit only the woman to take advantage

[28] Feije, *De Impedimentis,* n. 653.

[29] De Smet, *Betrothment and Marriage,* n. 817.

[30] Cappello, *De Sacramentis,* III, n. 260.

[31] *Cf.* Vlaming, *Praelectiones Juris Matrimonii,* II, n. 423.

[32] Rosset, *De Sacramento Matrimonii* (Paris, 1895), IV, n. 2572, apud Gasparri, *De Matrimonio,* n. 303, note 1.

[33] De Smet, *Betrothment and Marriage,* n. 815.

of the cause of *angustia loci* for without difficulty especially in these modern times, a man can more easily go in quest of a suitable partner. Moreover, the incidents supposed by Rosset [34] will not frequently transpire but when they should be verified, contrary to De Smet's definite stand, equity would sometimes demand that the cause be invoked in favor of the man.

Practical Application

From the time when the cause of *angustia loci* was first admitted, that is, sometime prior to the reign of Paul V (1605-1621) [35] it was admitted only for removing the impediments of consanguinity and affinity. But of what practical use is the cause of *angustia loci* today? How often will the petition arise asking that a woman be permitted to contract marriage with a man who is related to her within the forbidden degees of consanguinity and affinity because she finds it difficult to find a suitable husband elsewhere? When it does arise it can be disposed of according to the sense of the cause as contained in the wording of the Instruction of the Propaganda. But to make the cause of *angustia loci* of more practical value why should it not be used with reference to the impediments of mixed religion and disparity of cult? These two impediments are mentioned because in America their presence is of serious moment. If the cause of *angustia loci* can be extended to both of these impediments it would not be difficult to use it with reference to the minor impediments of spiritual relationship and public honesty. It would be difficult to suppose that the cause of *angustia loci* would be of great weight in petitioning for a dispensation from the impediment of age. Rather such an impediment would be dispensed from only for a most urgent reason,[36] *e. g.*, for the purpose of uniting two reigning families. Finally it would be more difficult to imagine the necessity of invoking the cause of *angustia loci* in obtaining dispensation from the dispensable impediments of vows or orders.

[34] Rosset, *De Sacramento Matrimonii,* 4, n. 2572, apud Gasparri, *De Matrimonio,* n. 303, note 1.

[35] De Justis, *De Dispensationibus Matrimonialibus,* L. III, c. 2.

[36] *Cf.* Gasparri, *De Matrimonio,* n. 499.

It seems that for all practical purposes the possibility need be established of using the cause of *angustia loci* for the impediments of disparity of cult and mixed religion. Some authors seem to fear that such an attempt might be made and specifically state that the cause must be used only regarding consanguinity and affinity.[37] Gasparri holds that the cause of *angustia loci* can be used as a cumulative cause for dispensing from the impediment of mixed religion.[38] He is silent on the possibility of its being used for disparity of cult. Putzer,[39] speaking rather indefinitely, says that it seems as though the cause of *angustia loci* need not entirely be ruled out in dispensing from disparity of cult, provided another cause is also present. Some authors can be found [40] who claim that while the cause of *angustia loci* is meant primarily as a reason for dispensing from the impediments of consanguinity and affinity it can be used by the woman when she finds it possible suitably to contract only among her relatives or among others *impeded in some other way* and in this latter instance the cause of *angustia loci* could be advanced for seeking a dispensation from the other impediment. The authors quoted do not distinguish the other impediments but simply say "impeded in another way," hence leaving the way open for mixed religion and disparity of cult.

In the preface of the Instruction, the Propaganda signifies its intention of enumerating "those principal causes which are accustomed to be held sufficient for obtaining matrimonial dispensations. . . ." Evidently it was not the purpose of the Propaganda to regard the causes in general as applying solely to the impediments of consanguinity and affinity. It is true, however, that in the phrasing of the cause of *angustia loci,* the impediments of cansanguinity and affinity form the apparent objects. This seems clear from the words " . . . *invenire nequeat, nisi consanguineum vel affinem.*" But it

[37] *E. g.,* De Smet, *Betrothment and Marriage,* n. 817; Farrugia, *De Matrimonio,* n. 99, 1; Vromant, *Jus Missionariorum,* V, *De Matrimonio,* n. 144.

[38] Gasparri, *De Matrimonio,* n. 448, 1°; so also Bangen, *De Sponsalibus et Matrimonio,* Tit. IV, p. 21.

[39] Putzer, *Commentarium in Facultates Apostolicas,* n. 219.

[40] Ballerini-Palmieri, 6, n. 1366; apud Payen, *De Matrimonio,* I, n. 740; M. Heiss, *De Matrimonio,* Tractatus V, p. 203.

seems unreasonable to limit the use of the cause to these two impediments. In many localities the woman will not find her marriage possibilities impeded through consanguinity and affinity but she will be restricted by some other impediment equally ecclesiastical. Why in the one case should the cause of *angustia loci* be admitted in order to free a woman from an impediment, for example, consanguinity or affinity, and not be admitted at least cumulatively in another case to free a woman from an impediment, for instance, mixed religion or disparity of cult, when the impediments in both instances have been established by the same ecclesastical authority?

For this reason it would seem that equity would prompt the transference of the cause of *angustia loci* from dispensation so seldom asked for, namely, from the impediments of consanguinity and affinity, and be applied to dispensations that are all too frequently sought, namely from the impediments of mixed religion and disparity of cult.

Hence the circumstances surrounding the application of the cause will change somewhat. Instead of making her choice between consanguineous and unequal suitors the woman will be faced with the alternative of either Catholic men who are perhaps beneath her in station, age, piety, morals and customs, or non-Catholic men with any of whom she might contract an equitable marriage. She is forced to do one of two things, either she must remain unmarried if she rejects any of the few Catholics in her locality or she must choose a non-Catholic.

It can easily be seen how, even traditionally, the cause of *angustia loci* should be regarded in the minds of European canonists as applying only to the impediments of consanguinity and affinity. In Europe mixed and disparate marriages are quite the exception.[41] On the other hand consanguineous and affined marriages are not uncommon. This condition exists through force of circumstance for in Europe communities are more compact. Very often the same families have lived in the town for countless generations. The population, too, of European towns is not in a state of flux so common in

[41] "Extra loca missionum facultas dispensandi ab hoc impedimento raro conceditur Ordinariis."—Gasparri, *De Matrimonio,* n. 593.

America. Due to these facts the woman in the European community will find that her marriageable possibilities exist only among her relatives. In America the woman is not placed in the midst of consanguineous and affined marriage choices but she will find her equitable marriage possibilities to be often among non-Catholics.

In the European situation the Church pleads the cause of equity. Every man and woman has the natural right to contract marriage unless he or she is impeded by the natural law and every man and woman has the right, too, to insist upon equitable unions. A man can negotiate an equitable union more easily than can the woman since he is not so strictly bound to one locality. For this reason the Church for centuries has recognized the cause of *angustia loci* for the woman and she has permitted the woman, who is surrounded by relatives, to use her natural right to an equitable marriage and to this end has dispensed because of narrowness of place from the impediments of cansanguinity and affinity.

May not a parallel condition exist for the American woman? She, too, has the natural right to an equitable marriage. Her choice of a husband is not limited because of the presence of relatives on the one hand and of unequal suitors on the other; but her choice is limited because of the large number of non-Catholics among whom she lives. In dispensing from the impediment of consanguinity the Church is permitted a marriage which, while it is not strictly against the law of nature,[42] nevertheless involves a certain repugnance to natural decency, especially if the relationship is of a closer degree. In dispensing from the impediments of mixed religion and disparity of cult the Church is permitting a marriage which is in no way contrary to the natural law, nor even against the divine law if the danger of perversion has been removed. Because the circumstances surrounding the life of the American woman are different than those in which the European woman lives, she should not be asked to marry unequally or to remain unmarried while the European woman is permitted to contract an equitable marriage with one who is bound by an impediment no less ecclesiastical than the impediments of mixed religion and disparity of cult.

[42] Except in the first degree of consanguinity in the direct line.

Only in the first degree of the direct line is consanguinity certainly an impediment of the natural law. In the first degree of the collateral line it is probably an impediment of the natural law.[43] Furthermore it might be said that dispensation from the impediments of mixed religion and disparity of cult, the danger of perversion being removed, are less repugnant to decency than dispensation from consanguinity and affinity since these approach more closely, as it were, the indispensable, that is the natural law.

Finally, it is not difficult to imagine instances in which *angustia loci* is the *only* reason that *can* be advanced for seeking a dispensation from disparity of cult or mixed religion. By way of example it could so happen that a woman finds herself one of a hundred Catholics living in a town having a population of five thousand inhabitants. She is limited in her choice of a husband and to contract suitably she must choose from among the non-Catholics. She therefore petitions a dispensation on the grounds of *angustia loci.* By her own admission she is marrying the non-Catholic simply because she cannot find a suitable partner among the few Catholics in the town. To make the case more strong it can be supposed that the woman is determined not to contract civilly or *coram ministello,* if the dispensation is denied. It can be argued, however, that there is very frequently danger of such marriages being contracted outside the Church. In this instance, however, it is certain that the woman will not so act. This being true the *only* reason that can truthfully be advanced is *angustia loci* and since the woman is so fervent in her faith, it would be unfair to advance the cause of danger of civil marriage or of marriage *coram ministello,* thus implying that the woman is weak in her faith which in this case is not true.

The purpose here is to establish the right of using at least cumulatively the cause of *angustia loci* for mixed and disparate marriages and to indicate that in some localities and in some instances the cause can be one of no little moment. If the possibility of using the cause of *angustia loci* with reference to the impediments of mixed religion and disparity of cult is admitted, there should be little

[43] *Cf.* Wahl, *The Matrimonial Impediments of Consanguinity and Affinity,* p. 28.

difficulty in applying the words of the Instruction to each individual case. The narrowness of the place, either absolute or relative, will be determined according to the principles already noted, namely, places of less than three hundred families or fifteen hundred inhabitants can claim absolute *angustia loci;* places having more than these allotted numbers are relatively small due to the particular inequality existing among the men of the locality and the woman who is desirous of contracting marriage.

As a practical illustration it can be supposed that a Catholic woman, desirous of marriage, lives in a small town. The Catholic population is lower than the allotted fifteen hundred. The few Catholic men whom she could marry are on an unequal plane with her. They may be older or younger than she, or they may be of a lower social stratum. She need not be forced into an unequal marriage nor is she to be restricted to a choice of one among three or four.[44] She has an inherent right to marriage which in the last analysis, cannot be taken from her. The right of the Church to establish matrimonial impediments is not being treated here. This right is granted. An attempt is being made to indicate that in a particular case a woman has a right to petition dispensation from an impediment which, unquestionably, the Church has a right to establish.

To return to the illustration being cited, it happens that the only eligible suitors in the town for this particular Catholic woman are to be found among the non-Catholics. It so happens too, in the final analysis, it is one particular non-Catholic whom the girl considers as her equal. The man in question is bound by the impediment of either mixed religion or disparity of cult. Usually a dispensation is not sought until the petitioner is ready to use it. In the instance under consideration the man and woman have probably contemplated marriage for some time past and they will not be easily turned from their purpose. The woman has been forced to seek dispensation *solely* because of *angustia loci.* It was practically imminent that she would become engaged to a man bound either by the impediment of mixed religion or disparity of cult. The cause of *angustia loci* in this case is verified and if in curial practice the Holy See will not

[44] Sanchez, *De Matrimonio,* L. VIII, disput. 19, n. 14.

recognize it as the motivating cause, it should at least be recognized as having impulsive value.

The illustration as cited is by no means of rare occurrence. In such instances why should not the cause of *angustia loci* be admitted, at least cumulatively, for removing the impediments of mixed religion or disparity of cult? By a parallel the woman herself sought this marriage only because the conditions necessary for the cause were verified, that is, she was literally forced to choose such a union or remain unmarried. Only in the event that dispensation would be denied for the cause of *angustia loci* does another motivating cause arrive, namely, danger of a civil marriage or marriage *coram ministello*.

As has been said, the cause must be applied according to the norms indicated by the Instruction and the opinions of reputable authors. It seems but equitable that the Catholic women living in small towns should be permitted to advance the cause of *angustia loci,* at least as a cumulative cause, if they find it difficult or impossible to contract suitably. Of course it is understood that the dispensation should be granted only when danger of perversion has been removed.[45] But the cause of *angustia loci* can be invoked in those places of over fifteen hundred inhabitants only when the cause is verified relatively, as for instance, the case of a woman wishing to marry within a national group.

It would seem however that in permitting the use of the cause in suburban districts, a more strict accounting should be in order. Reputable canonists permitted the cause in such a place when it was removed three quarters of a mile or a twenty minute journey in distance from the city of which it was a part. Considering the modern means of transportation and communication, the people living in surburban communities are no longer so isolated from the parent city. Their modes of living can be considered. If they are removed from the city only the distance of three-quarters of a mile and if their economic and social life is so intimately bound up with the city so as, economically and socially, to be one with the city, there seems little grounds for admitting *angustia loci.* On the other hand, how-

[45] *Cf.* Canon 1060.

ever, each case should be examined for it must be admitted from the opinion of authors no woman is bound to seek a husband. The Instruction states that she must find difficulty in leaving home. Perhaps in these times this difficulty is reduced to a minimum for a woman living in a suburban community. In fact for the most part the modern social life of a neighboring community very largely turns toward the larger city and in this way it can scarcely be said that a woman has broken the home ties. In other words the breaking of home ties is really verified when a woman living in a distinct community betakes herself into a larger one than in the case of the surburban woman who claims that she is being forced to leave home when it is suggested to her that she might contract a suitable marriage in the city adjoining her community. But in general, even here the woman can hold that she herself is not bound to go in quest of a husband.

2. *Super-adult Age. (Aetas super adulta)*

The cause of super-adult age is verified if the woman, having completed the age of twenty-four years, has not yet found a man of worthy condition whom she might marry. This cause *per se,* however, cannot be used in the case of a widow who is seeking remarriage.[46]

At the first glance it would seem that this cause is more or less a modification of the cause of *angustia loci.* There is, however, little correlation. In the cause of super-adult age there is simply placed the condition that the woman has completed the twenty-fourth year of her age and has not yet found a worthy man whom she might marry. Nothing is said of the woman's inability to find a worthy partner as in the cause of *angustia loci; de facto* it is only necessary that she has not found a worthy suitor.[47] This simple requisite eliminates the necessity of searching the place for a suitable spouse. And further, the use of the cause need not be restricted to those places that have less than three hundred families or fifteen hundred inhabitants.[48] For determining the application of the cause of super-

[46] S. C. P. F., Instruction, 9 May, 1877, n. 2—*Collect. P. F.*, n. 1470.

[47] *Cf.* Feije, *De Impedimentis,* n. 664.

[48] Gasparri, *De Matrimonio,* n. 304, note 1.

adult age, however, the equality or inequality of the suitors is to be judged as in the case of *angustia loci, e. g.*, as to age, customs, morals and the like.

The prime reason for admitting the cause of super-adult age lies in the desire of the Church to remove from the woman the probability of her remaining unmarried and the consequent danger of incontinency if she is forced to live an unmarried life.[49]

In the first place the woman seeking dispensation on the ground of super-adult age must have completed twenty-four years of her life. [50] Although Vlaming,[51] claims that a bishop would invalidly act by virtue of an indult in dispensing for this cause a woman who was lacking even an hour of completing her twenty-fourth year, it seems safe enough to follow Gasparri,[52] and hold that with another just cause it suffices that the woman has begun the twenty-fourth year of her life. A woman therefore is said to be of super-adult age if she is over twenty-four years old and the cause can be invoked in her favor until she has attained the age of forty.[53] Some authors, however, hold that a woman who has passed the age of forty may allege the cause of super-adult age.[54] The greater weight of opinion, however, seems to be on the negative side. At any rate, when a woman over twenty-four invokes the cause, her exact age need not be stated in the petition, although if it is stated, it will react favorably to her.[55] In practice, however, this may not always be true since very often the baptismal certificate of the woman must be attached to the petition for dispensation. This is a chancery ruling in some places,[56] and it must be admitted that the practice has its merits.

The second requisite necessary for verifying the cause of super-

[49] Payen, *De Matrimonio,* I, n. 741, n. 2.

[50] Farrugia, *De Matrimonio,* n. 99, p. 192. An exception can be made for a woman bereft of her parents.

[51] *Praelectiones Juris Matrimonii,* II, n. 624.

[52] Gasparri, *De Matrimonio,* n. 304, note 1.

[53] Payen, *De Matrimonio,* I, n. 741; Vlaming, *Praelectiones Juris Matrimonii,* II, n. 624; De Smet, *Betrothment and Marriage,* II, n. 818.

[54] De Justis, *De Dispensationibus Matrimonialibus,* L. III, c. 8, n. 16-22.

[55] *Cf.* Feije, *De Impedimentis,* n. 664.

[56] *E. g.*, in Brussels; *cf.* De Smet, *Betrothment and Marriage,* III, n. 818, note 3.

adult age is the fact that the woman has not found a worthy partner up to the time when she has attained or passed the age of twenty-four years. As has been previously noted it is not necessary in alleging this cause that the woman is ***unable to find*** a worthy man. The cause can be advanced if up to this time she has not *found* one; in other words because she is somewhat beyond the usual age at which a woman of her locality marries she is faced with the alternative of accepting a suitor below her in station, or if she refuses him, she must face the probability of remaining unmarried with the consequent danger of incontinency. The only solution to her problem lies in the benignity of the Church in granting dispensation that she might contract an equitable marriage with a man who is otherwise laboring under some matrimonial impediment.

Since, as has been said, it is not necessary for verifying the cause that the woman was unable to find a man of worthy station, the use of the cause of super-adult age need not be restricted to those places having less than three hundred families or fifteen hundred inhabitants.[57] It need only be determined that the only unimpeded suitors have been, or are likely to be, men who are beneath her in station. To be exact even this condition need not be an absolute requisite for the validity of a dispensation on the ground of super-adult age. According to a reply of the Sacred Penitentiary it need not be asked and proved that the super-adult woman has not up to this time found a man of like condition whom she might marry; it is sufficient that she has certainly attained super-adult age.[58] Hence it would seem that the fact that the woman has remained unmarried after her twenty-fourth year is more of a prime consideration than the fact that prior to that time she may have had opportunities to contract an equitable marriage and may have rejected the opportunities. This is the interpretation that Gasparri places on the response of the Sacred Penitentiary.[59] In this connection some authors [60] hold that if a woman has ever had the opportunity to con-

[57] S. Poenit., Response, 5 April, 1902—*Collect. P. F.*, n. 2134.

[58] *Cf.* S. Poenit., Response, 5 April, 1902—*Collect. P. F.*, n. 2134.

[59] Gasparri, *De Matrimonio*, n. 304, note 1.

[60] Corradus, *Praxis Dispensationum Apostolicarum*, L. VII, c. 2, n. 93; Vlaming, *Praelectiones Juris Matrimonii*, II, n. 424c.

tract an equitable marriage and has rejected it, the cause of super-adult age is not verified. This opinion in the estimation of some authors[61] admits of a variation, namely, if once or many times the woman has rejected the proposals for an equitable marriage while harboring the thought of leading a celibate life, the cause of super-adult age is verified if afterward she decides to enter the married state. Other authors, however,[62] hold the opinion, which they call probable, that a refusal on the part of the woman before she has attained the age of twenty-four in no way makes her ineligible for later advancing the cause of super-adult age. This seems the more reasonable opinion since the prime purpose of the cause is to make it possible for a woman to remove herself from the probability of remaining unmarried with the consequent danger of incontinency. She may have refused the equitable marriage proposals without foreseeing that more such proposals would not be given her. As every woman (and man) has the inherent right to marriage, so also can she use or refuse that right. In the past the woman under consideration was not bound to accept any of the equitable proposals and when later she finds it impossible to receive such proposals from suitable and unimpeded men, she should not be denied the use of the cause of super-adult age. If she is, then she is exposed to the probability of remaining unmarried with the consequent danger of incontinency, and it is these two evils that the cause is designed to avert. Furthermore, if the woman has previously refused the opportunity of an equitable marriage and later obtains dispensation for the cause of super-adult age without mentioning this fact in the petition, the dispensation is valid from the modern discipline of the Holy See.[63]

The authors agree that the cause of super-adult age cannot be invoked by a woman before she has attained the age of twenty-four years unless other just causes are also had. In this event the cause

[61] Vlaming, *Praelectiones Juris Matrimonii,* II, n. 424.

[62] De Justis, *De Dispensationibus Matrimonialibus,* L. III, c. 8, n. 30 sq.; Giovine, *De Dispensationibus Matrimonialibus,* t. II, p. 226, n. 6; Gasparri, *De Matrimonio,* n. 304, note 1; Cappello, *De Sacramentis,* III, n. 261.

[63] Cappello, *De Sacramentis,* III, n. 261, c; Gasparri, *De Matrimonio,* 304, note 1.

of super-adult age would be only an impulsive cause or would aid in forming an aggregate motivating cause. The authors who mention the point are likewise agreed that the cause of super-adult age is a sufficient cause in the case of a woman, below the age of twenty-four, who has been bereft of one of her parents, especially her mother, or with more reason, if she has lost both parents.[64] It can be seen that in such an instance the Church regards the welfare of the woman and does not strictly adhere to the fulfillment of the age limit. Prior to her parents' death the girl had a home and someone to care for her needs. After her bereavement this support was withdrawn and because of the absence of parental influence should more readily be exposed to the danger of incontinence. For this reason it is permitted to her to plead super-adult age. The authors make no attempt at determining how long prior to the age of twenty-four the cause of super-adult age can be invoked in such cases. For the most part under such circumstances it seems that the approaching super-adult age of the woman would be considered equally with the fact of her orphaned state. Indeed, if anything, the fact that she is deprived of the care and support to which she is accustomed would in reality work more in her favor than her proximity to super-adult age. This seems probable since the bereavement of parents forms in itself a canonical reason for dispensation.[65] In general, however, it can be said that the closer the woman is to the age of twenty-four the greater should be the weight of the cause in her favor.

From the words of the Instruction [66] it is noted that the cause of super-adult age cannot be invoked for a widow who desires remarriage. But the authors have taken this to mean that the cause in itself is insufficient for obtaining a dispensation for a widow who contemplates such action. But it can be used to advantage when other causes can be advanced in the widow's case. If she is of *aetas florens,* namely to the age of twenty-five, or of *aetas junior,*

[64] Gasparri, *De Matrimonio,* n. 304, note 1; Cappello, *De Sacramentis,* III, n. 261f.

[65] Dataria Apostolica Causae Canonicae Ordinariae Matrimonialium dispensationum sufficientes sive conjunctae plures, sive solae et aliarum normae.—*A. S. S.,* XXXIV, p. 34.

[66] S. C. P. F., Instruction, 9 May, 1877, n. 2—*Collect. P. F.,* n. 1470.

namely to the age of thirty, the danger of incontinency is present for her and this, together with the cause of super-adult age, can form an aggregate motivating cause. Or oftentimes the *bonum prolis* is a fact worthy of consideration when applying the cause of super-adult age in a widow's petition for dispensation from an impediment.[67]

Practical Application

Naturally it is to be asked of what value and weight is the canonical cause of super-adult age. It would be difficult to make a definite statement in this regard. *Per se* the cause of super-adult age seems to be a *causa minoris ponderis*.[68] Hence its value will depend more or less on the circumstances of the case for which its application is invoked. Evidently the Church in fixing the determinant for super-adult age at twenty-four years attempted to strike a medium which could more or less apply to the entire world. In those countries where it is customary for a woman to marry at an early age, the fact that she has attained the age of twenty-four and is still unmarried is quite a positive indication that she will continue unmarried. In such an instance the cause of super-adult age can be of significant consideration and if an attempt is made to classify this cause it can be a very probable impulsive cause or even a final cause in dispensing from the less grave impediments.[69] In the more grave impediments, however, in the second degree of consanguinity the cause of super-adult age does not seem sufficient in itself.[70] The cause, however, becomes more grave in proportion to the increasing age of the woman and the circumstances of various places and persons.[71] As a practical observation it might be said that in accordance with our local customs a woman who has but recently attained the super-adult age of twenty-four years need not *per se* be considered as

[67] *Cf.* Gasparri, *De Matrimonio,* n. 304, note 1; Cappello, *De Sacramentis,* III, n. 261g; Payen, *De Matrimonio,* I, n. 741, n. 1; Wernz-Vidal, *Jus Matrimoniale,* V, n. 432, note 105.

[68] Chelodi, *Jus Matrimoniale,* n. 46.

[69] *Cf.* Canon 1042.

[70] *Cf.* Rosset, *De Sacramento Matrimonii,* 4, n. 2574, apud Payen, *De Matrimonio,* I, n. 741.

[71] Gasparri, *De Matrimonio,* n. 304, note 1.

facing the probable danger of remaining unmarried since even the average age at which a woman marries is not very much below the age of twenty-four years. Hence it does not seem that the cause of super-adult age can be more than an impulsive cause (and moreover of little weight) until the woman has reached a more advanced age, *e.g.*, twenty-eight to thirty years. When the age of thirty years has been attained there should be no doubt as to the cause being at least of impulsive value.[72] In practice, however, since the cause of super-adult age is a *causa minoris ponderis*,[73] it is not used except with other causes, *e.g.*, with the cause of *angustia loci* and the good morals of both the *orator* and the *oratrix*. Furthermore, there is no reason to hold that the cause of *aetas super adulta* cannot be invoked, at least impulsively, for seeking dispensation from any of the matrimonial impediments. This can be judged from the words of the prologue to the Instruction on canonical causes issued by the Propaganda in 1877,[74] and from the tenor of the words when the specific cause is mentioned in the body of the Instruction. In the prologue the Propaganda states that an enumeration of the "principal causes for matrimonial dispensations" will be attempted. Hence in general the causes are not intended as applying only to the impediments of consanguinity and affinity. In treating specifically of the cause of super-adult age the Propaganda in no way infers that the cause is intended for dispensation from any particular impediment. In commenting on the cause of super-adult age Giovine [75] takes it for granted that its use is not confiined solely to consanguinity. He says that the cause might be used by a woman in seeking dispensation for contracting with a relative or with another who might be laboring under an *impediment*.

3. *Lack of Proper Dowry (Incompetentia dotis)*

The canonical cause of want of or insufficiency of dowry is

[72] *Cf.* Rosset, *De Sacramento Matrimonii*, 4, n. 2574, apud Payen, *De Matrimonio*, I, n. 741.

[73] Chelodi, *Jus Matrimoniale*, n. 46.

[74] S. C. P. F., Instruction, 9 May, 1877, n. 2—*Collect. P. F.*, n. 1470.

[75] Giovine, *De Dispensationibus Matrimonialibus*, t. 1, p. 226, n. 6.

verified if the woman is not in actual possession of a sufficient dowry to enable her to marry, in the place in which she is living, a man of like position who is unrelated to her either by consanguinity or affinity. This cause is the more forceful, if the woman entirely lacks a dowry and a relative by blood or marriage is willing to marry her or is prepared suitably to dower her.[76] In those countries in which the dotal system exists, the dowry is understood to mean those things which are given to the husband, by the bride or by another in the bride's name, for sustaining the burdens of the married state. These goods, during the time of the marriage, are to be administered by the husband and if the marriage is dissolved the goods are to return to the woman or her heirs.[77] In a less complex aspect the dowry, in places not having a dotal system, is simply those goods which the woman brings with her for sustaining the common burdens of the married state. The right of administering them and their ultimate disposition is of no consideration.[78] In fact the dowry used in the sense of its being that property which the wife brings to her husband on marriage remains a part of the separate property of the wife.[79]

With this distinction in mind it can be said that from the ecclesiastical viewpoint the woman lacks a proper dowry when her poverty is so pronounced that she can give little or no fortune to the man she would marry. In those countries in which it is customary for the woman to furnish a dowry, this system can present a serious problem. A man would be hesitant in taking an undowered woman. The woman herself would face the probability of remaining unmarried or of being forced to marry beneath her station. The Church wishes to avert these evils and if the woman can find a man who is related to her by blood or marriage living in her own town who is willing to marry her regardless of her lack of dowry or is even willing to dower her himself, the woman can seek dispensation from the impediments of consanguinity or affinity for the canonical

[76] S. C. P. F., Instruction, 9 May, 1877, n. 2—*Collect. P. F.*, n. 1470.

[77] Vlaming, *Praelectiones Juris Matrimonii*, II, n. 425d, note 1.

[78] Cappello, *De Sacramentis*, III, n. 262a; Prümmer, *Manuale Theologiae Moralis*, III, n. 862.

[79] Ballentine's Law Dictionary, p. 407.

cause of lack of proper dowry. The cause can be alleged if it is established that *hic et nunc* the woman does not possess a sufficient dowry. The certain hope of obtaining a fortune in the future would not exclude the use of the cause. Hence if the woman will come into an inheritance of her own on the death of her parents or if they, for some reason, are unwilling or unable to dower the daughter without their being reduced to poverty, or finally if someone else has promised to endow the woman, but the woman, on her part, cannot show a legal claim to the promised dowry, then in any of these cases the woman can plead lack of proper dowry.[80] But if the woman, from agreement or law, can on instituting civil proceedings obtain a dowry from her parents or from some other source, she cannot claim a lack of proper dowry.[81] The cause can likewise be alleged if, for some reason, even a dishonest one, the woman has renounced a dowry.[82] She should not, however, have rejected her dowry for the express purpose of obtaining a dispensation *propter incompetentiam dotis*. If she has, this fact should be noted in the petition for dispensation. If, however, it is not noted and the dispensation is granted, the dispensation is valid.[83] If, however, the woman has falsely alleged lack of dowry, the dispensation under the new law is valid if it concerns an impediment of a minor degree; *e.g.*, consanguinity in the third degree of the collateral line; [84] if it concerns an impediment of a major degree, *e.g.*, consanguinity in the second degree of the collateral line, the dispensation is null by subreption.[85] Because of the lack of proper dowry the woman must find that she is able to contract an equitable union in the place in which she lives

[80] Sanchez, *De Matrimonio,* L. VIII, disput. 19, n. 25; Giovine, *De Dispensationibus Matrimonialibus,* I, p. 373, sq. et II, p. 211 sq.; De Justis, *De Dispensationibus Matrimonialibus,* III, c. 3, n. 43; Gasparri, *De Matrimonio,* n. 305. note 1.

[81] Vlaming, *Praelectiones Juris Matrimonii,* II, n. 425a.

[82] Sanchez, *De Matrimonio,* L. VIII, disput. n. 26; De Justis, *De Dispensationibus Matrimonialibus,* L. III, c. 3, n. 60; Feije, *De Impedimentis et Dispensationibus Matrimonialibus,* n. 657.

[83] Feije, *De Impedimentis,* n. 656 and n. 659; Gasparri, *De Matrimonio,* n. 305, note 1, and n. 342; Cappello, *De Sacramentis,* III, n. 260 and n. 262.

[84] Canon 1042, § 1.

[85] Canon 40.

only with a man related to her within the prohibited degrees of consanguinity or affinity. There is a certain lenient characteristic in this legislation. In the first place the disparity of condition between the woman and the various men of the place need not be subjected to exact scrutiny. That disparity admitted in applying the causes of *angustia loci* and of *aetas super-adulta* will also be admitted for this cause. In fact the disparity of condition may lean rather toward the woman. She may be able, considering her family position, to offer a substantial dowry but because she may be crippled or quarrelsome or defamed she finds it impossible equitably to contract a marriage outside her family.[86] In such an instance lack of dowry need not be alleged. A more exact statement of the case can be described by the words: because of insufficient dowry.

Furthermore, it need only be necessary that no eligible, unimpeded men can be found in the place in which the woman lives. Because of the custom of the locality it so happens that they cannot be prevailed upon to accept undowered wives. The cause of lack of or insufficient dowry cannot be denied if in another locality other than her own, the woman can find an equtable partner or that because of the custom of the locality [87] her small dowry is held entirely sufficient. This is clear from the words of the Instruction: "Qui neque consanguineus neque affinis sit, nubere possit *in proprio loco,* in quo commoratur." [88]

The petition for dispensation for the cause of lack of or insufficiency of dowry can be drafted in four different ways: [89]

1. *Propter incompetentiam dotis,* namely when the woman has a small dowry and the prospective husband is prepared both to inher in marriage.

2. *Propter dotem cum augmento,* namely when the woman has a small dowry and the prospective husband is prepared to both increase the woman's small dowry and to accept her in marriage.

3. When another increases the dowry.

[86] Feije, *De Impedimentis,* n. 656.

[87] For the woman is never forced to leave home for the purpose of seeking a husband.

[88] S. C. P. F., Instruction, 9 May, 1877, n. 3—*Collect. P. F.,* n. 1470.

[89] *Cf.* Vlaming, *Praelectiones Juris Matrimonii,* II, n. 425, II.

4. *Pro indotata,* namely when the woman is entirely destitute of a dowry and the man is willing to accept her in this condition.

The exactness in applying these phrases to various cases regards rather the impulsive than the final cause.[90] Hence if a woman can truthfully claim insufficiency of dowry while in reality she claims that she is entirely without dowry, the dispensation is valid.[91]

Practical Application

Only in those countries in which the dotal system exists will the cause of lack or insufficiency of dowry be of value. In this regard it is to be remembered that in civil law dotal property and the dower are distinct. That property is known as dotal property which the wife brings to the husband to assist him in bearing the expenses of the marital establishment.[92] The dower in American civil law is the legal right or interest which the wife acquires by marriage in the real estate of her husband.[93]

When canon law speaks of *deficientia aut incompetentia dotis,* it is the dotal property known to civil law to which reference is made. In some countries, whether sanctioned by both custom and law or by custom alone, it so happens that when a man seeks a wife the wealth of the woman's father is a consideration. If the father is a man of means it is quite natural that the prospective bridegroom will expect that his prospective bride will bring him a fair amount of dotal property. If the woman's father is not so well situated a smaller amount can be agreed upon. Finally, if the father is without means the woman is in danger of having no suitors at all to seek her in marriage and she must remain unmarried. Hence the Church admits the cause of deficiency or incompetence of dowry in those countries in which such prenuptial customs exist.

In such instances the question naturally arises as to what impediments the cause can be applied for seeking a dispensation. From the words found in the Instruction the cause is to be considered only

90 Cappello, *De Sacramentis,* III, n. 262d.

91 Canon 1054.

92 Ballentine's Law Dictionary, p. 405.

93 Ballentine's Law Dictionary, p. 407.

in regard to the impediments of consanguinity and affinity.[94] Since it is a canonical cause for dispensation, however, there is no reason why it cannot be applied to all impediments although with unequal weight. Moreover, it is a cause of private nature and of lesser weight but it can be admitted as an impulsive cause, for dispensing from other impediments, *e. g.*, from mixed religion.[95] But since the authors, in treating the cause, have adhered to the words of the Instruction, they have regarded it as applying primarily to the impediments of consanguinity and affinity and have made suggestions for its application only in favor of these two impediments. Hence it can be found that the cause, when the woman entirely lacks dowry, will suffice in the opinion of some authors for obtaining a dispensation from the impediment of consanguinity in the second degree, even though it perhaps touches the first degree especially when other causes concur.[96] Other authors,[97] hold that the cause *seems* to be sufficient in itself when the woman is entirely without dowry.

When the woman has a small but insufficient dowry the cause can be advanced for dispensation from the impediment of consanguinity in the third degree of the equal line. When the prospective husband, himself or by another, increases the small dowry of the woman, then the cause can be admitted for the third degree of consanguinity either equal or touching the second.[98]

But this cause of insufficiency of dowry must not be invoked for removing the impediment of consanguinity in the first degree of the collateral line mixed with the second. The use of such a cause for removing such an impediment was explicitly forbidden in an instruction issued by the Sacred Congregation of the Sacraments on August 1, 1931.[99] In this instruction the Congregation calls attention to the fact that petitions for dispensation in such close degrees

[94] S. C. P. F., Instruction, 9 May, 1877, n. 3—*Collect. P. F.*, n. 1470.

[95] Gasparri, *De Matrimonio*, n. 448.

[96] Feije, *De Impedimentis*, n. 660; Vlaming, *Praelectiones Juris Matrimonii*, II, n. 425d.

[97] Rosset, 4, n. 2579, sq. et Ballerini-Palmieri, 6, n. 1366, apud Payen, *De Matrimonio*, I, n. 742.

[98] Vlaming, *Praelectiones Juris Matrimonii*, II, n. 425.

[99] *A. A. S.*, XXIII (1931), 413.

of consanguinity are rapidly increasing and since marriages in such close degrees of kindred often result in impairment to family life spiritually, temporally and physically, the Holy See is determined to check this evil and will in the future permit such marriages only for such grave causes as the prevention of notable scandal, the settlement of important questions affecting the succession of property or the relief of involved or very distressing family conditions. Because the Holy See has seen fit to rule out such causes as are admitted for other impediments even of a major grade, as for example the cause of *angustia loci* or insufficiency of dowry, it would seem that a complete change of legislation has taken place for formerly these causes could at times be final causes in petitioning dispensation in even the closer degrees of consanguinity.

As has been remarked, this cause of *deficentia aut incompetentia dotis* is of prime value only in those countries where the dowry forms more or less a prenuptial requisite and in these places an instance could often arise where such a cause could be truly motivating. In other places, for instance in America, it can at best be only an impulsive cause. Here it would apply more properly in the case of a poor girl who has the opportunity of contracting an equitable marriage and who at the same time can invoke the causes of *angustia loci* and *aetas super-adulta*. Payen, however, says in those places in which the woman is given no dotal property the cause is entirely without weight.[100]

4. Legal Litigation (Propter lites)

The fourth cause enumerated by the Propaganda reads: A lawsuit already begun with regard to an inheritance or the serious or imminent danger of such proceedings. If the woman is engaged in a lawsuit about an important inheritance and no one is willing to take the matter in hand and defray the expenses, except the man who wishes to marry her, it is customary to grant a dispensation; for the general good demands that legal proceedings should not be prolonged. Intimately related with this cause is that of a legally contested dowry, when a woman has no one else willing to assist her

[100] Payen, *De Matrimonio,* I, n. 742.

in recovering the property. This cause, however, suffices for only the remote degrees.[101]

From the closing sentence with which this cause *propter lites* is set forth by the Propaganda, it is to be inferred that the cause is of little moment. Gasparri,[102] notes that according to the *Praxis Datariae*, n. 95, the cause is a grave one because it is destined both to aid the woman lest she be unjustly deprived of her inheritance or dotal property and to avert scandal and sin which usually arise from such legal contests.

In order to emphasize the various elements of the cause *propter lites* a closer scrutiny can be given to the words through which the cause is stated. The first requisite that must be present before the application of the cause can be considered is the fact of a lawsuit either already begun or dangerously imminent. The object of the lawsuit is either an inheritance or dotal property. To all intents and purposes this is only a specific statement of the elements involved.[103] The next requisite for the cause is found in the fact that the only one whom the woman can interest in the legal proceedings is the man whom she wishes to marry. The man is impeded in some way from marrying the woman, else there would be no need for seeking a dispensation. For such reasons the Church is accustomed to grant the petitioned dispensation for, having the general well-being in mind, she is always solicitous lest lawsuits be unduly prolonged.[104] Before the cause can be applied in these cases it is to be determined whether the man whom the woman wishes to marry is really interested in her plight, whether he is capable of being of aid to her, *e. g.*, whether he is wealthy or influential enough to assume the expenses of the suit and whether his presence in the case is as essential as it is claimed to be, *i. e.*, whether someone else easily can be found who is able and willing to aid her.[105]

Since this cause in given circumstances can assume grave pro-

[101] S. C. P. F., Instruction, 9 May, 1877, n. 4—*Collect. P. F.*, n. 1470; S. C. Sacr. Instruction, 1 August, 1931—*A. A. S.*, XXIII (1931), 413.

[102] Gasparri, *De Matrimonio*, n. 306, note 2.

[103] *Cf.* Chelodi, *Jus Matrimoniale*, n. 46.

[104] C. 2, *de judiciis*, II, 2, in Clem.

[105] *Cf.* Gasparri, *De Matrimonio*, n. 306, note 2.

portions and is recognized as a grave cause by the *praxis* of the Apostolic Dataria, it should be of value in dispensing from any of the matrimonial impediments. Its strength in dispensing from the graver impediments should be determined in accordance with gravity of the case itself, *e. g.*, whether all the requisites for the application of the cause are present, whether the case is of grave proportions and whether the case can be solved only through the application of the cause.

In practice the cause will be rarely invoked in our local situations especially with regard to gaining possession of an involved dotal property since dotal property has no place as a prenuptial requisite. It could, however, more often happen that a widow is involved in a lawsuit and the only aid that she can obtain is from the impeded man whom she desires to marry.[106]

5. Poverty of a Widow (Paupertas viduae)

When a woman is burdened with a numerous offspring her state of poverty can constitute a canonical cause for removing an impediment to a marriage with some man who promises to care for her and her children. Sometimes also a widow is dispensed simply because she is young and in danger of incontinency.[107]

This cause of poverty of the widow is *per se* a *causa gravis*,[108] and according to circumstances can become more grave.[109] The primary design of this cause regards the welfare of the children instead of being concerned with the well-being of the adults involved.[110] The secondary reason for the cause lies in the danger of incontinency on the part of the widow because of her youthfulness.[111]

For the verification of this cause, then, according to the sense of the Instruction, it is necessary that the woman involved is a widow who has children born of a lawful marriage and not an un-

106 *Cf.* Payen, *De Matrimonio,* I, n. 743.

107 S. C. P. F., Instruction, 9 May, 1877, n. 5—*Collect. P. F.*, n. 1470.

108 Chelodi, *Jus Matrimoniale,* n. 46.

109 Zitelli, *Apparatus Juris Ecclesiastici,* p. 64.

110 Payen, *De Matrimonio,* I. n. 744; De Smet, *Betrothment and Marriage,* II, n. 821.

111 De Smet, *Betrothment and Marriage,* II, n. 821.

married woman who has an illegitimate child.[112] While the cause is canonical only in the case of a widow, the Holy See at the present time is not adverse to the use of this cause in favor of a widower although he may have but one child. It seems that through the use of this cause the Church desires to restore broken homes and hence is willing to grant a dispensation in favor of a widower.[113]

A woman having at least three or four children is said to have a "numerous offspring." [114] In the average case such a mother will find it difficult to care for and educate the children and if she has the opportunity to contract an equitable marriage with a man, who, however, is bound by some impediment, the Church is accustomed to grant dispensation from the impediment. In so acting the Church is desirous of restoring to the children a home that was probably broken through the death of their father. The fact that she is burdened with many children works to the advantage of the woman because the cause increases in weight in accordance with the number of the children and their youthful age. The application of the cause unquestionably comes in the case of a widow who is poor and who has a number of children to provide for and educate. But the absence of poverty does not imply that the cause cannot be invoked for oftentimes a dispensation is given even if the woman is not poor for the cause is supposed to work to the good of the children.[115] A woman may have sufficient means to give her children the proper care but it often happens that a suitable foster-father lends a stable and pleasing atmosphere to a home.

Through the sense of the Instruction the woman is supposed to be in poverty and this fact makes it difficult for her to find a husband who will relieve her of her poverty. But again the woman may not be poor and she may have only one child but because of other circumstances, for example, she may be in ill health, or she may be young and faced with the danger of incontinency, there is strong

[112] Feije, *De Impedimentis*, n. 663; De Smet, *Betrothment and Marriage*, II, n. 821.

[113] Payen, *De Matrimonio*, I, n. 744; De Smet, *Betrothment and Marriage*, II, n. 821.

[114] Payen, *De Matrimonio*, I, n. 744; Cappello, *De Sacramentis*, III, n. 264b.

[115] Chelodi, *Jus Matrimoniale*, n. 46.

reason why the dispensation should be granted.[116] In such instances the primary end for which the cause was designed, namely, the good of the children, is supported by the secondary end, namely the physical and temporal welfare of the mother.

In applying for a dispensation with the cause of poverty it is necessary to mention the number of children and their respective ages.[117]

Practical Application

Since the cause of *paupertas viduae* is by common opinion [118] to be enumerated among the canonical causes that are sufficiently grave, the practical value of the cause is not to be questioned. The cause becomes especially grave in cases where the widow is poor, where the children are numerous and have not yet reached the age of majority and where, because of the youthfulness of the woman, the danger of incontinency on her part is present.[119] No attempt should be made to confine its use within certain limits. It is without question a grave cause and, according to circumstances, should be admitted, when its use is applicable, for all impediments from which the Church is accustomed to dispense. Its gravity can be inferred from the fact that it seems to be a common opinion that the cause of *paupertas viduae* is certainly sufficient for dispensation from the impediment of consanguinity in the third degree of the collateral line touching the second.[120] In fact it is a final cause for obtaining dispensation from the impediment of affinity in the first degree of the collateral line especially when the widow is poor and youthful, when she has a large family to care for and when she is bereaved of her parents.[121]

[116] Feije, *De Impedimentis,* n. 663; De Smet, *Betrothment and Marriage,* n. 821.

[117] Vlaming, *Praelectiones Juris Matrimonii,* II, n. 427a.

[118] Chelodi, *Jus Matrimoniale,* n. 46; Gasparri, n. 307, n. 1; Payen, *De Matrimonio,* I, n. 744; De Smet, *Betrothment and Marriage,* n. 821; Vlaming, *Praelectiones Juris Matrimonii,* II, n. 427.

[119] Payen, *De Matrimonio,* I, n. 744.

[120] Vlaming, *Praelectiones Juris Matrimonii,* II, 427d; Bangen, *De Sponsalibus,* p. 187; Feije, *De Impedimentis,* n. 664.

[121] Bangen, *De Sponsalibus,* p. 187; Feije, *De Impedimentis,* n. 664; Vlaming, *Praelectiones Juris Matrimonii,* II, n. 427d.

Under prevailing modern conditions some of the canonical causes advanced from authoritative sources are more or less outmoded. This is by no means true of the cause *paupertas viduae,* since poverty is an inherent characteristic of every age and period. So from the practical viewpoint, the cause of *paupertas viduae* can frequently be invoked as a canonical cause for dispensation especially in rural communities. The case is by no means rare for a woman to seek dispensation to marry the brother of her deceased husband. Oftentimes the woman is poor, has a large family and the only one whom she can find to marry is the man who is laboring under the impediment of affinity in the first degree of the collateral line. This case is particularly aggravated if the man and woman happen to be occupying the same house.[122] Or again it can often happen in rural communities that the woman, on the death of her husband, finds it difficult to manage the farm on which she is living with her large family. It may so happen that she is desirous of contracting marriage with a man who has been caring for her farming interests since the death of her husband and who may be bound by some matrimonial impediment. In such cases it rarely happens that the Church will deny the dispensation sought even if it is a question of dispensation from the graver impediments.[123] From the situations described it need not be inferred that the cause of *paupertas viduae* is applicable only to cases originating in rural communities. A widow's poverty coupled with the probability of incontinency on her part can be a sad plight regardless of locality. In applying the cause it is to be borne in mind that the cause is designed primarily for the aid of the children involved. If, through their mother's remarriage, their spiritual and temporal welfare will be more assured, then the cause of *paupertas viduae* should be a weighty one and should add much in obtaining the dispensation that is being sought.

Finally it should be noted that there is no phrasing in the Instruction which would limit the use of the cause to the impediments of consanguinity and affinity.[124] The cause, *per se,* is grave and

[122] Bangen, *De Sponsalibus,* p. 187.

[123] Canon 1042; Bangen, *De Sponsalibus,* p. 188.

[124] S. C. P. F., Instruction, 9 May, 1877, n. 5—*Collect. P. F.,* n. 1470.

there seems to be no intrinsic reason why its use cannot be extended, *servatis servandis,* to any impediment placed by ecclesiastical law. In our local conditions the cause will frequently be invoked for obtaining dispensation from the impediments of mixed religion and disparity of cult. If the danger of perversion has been removed and the other conditions required by law have been complied with, it would seem that the cause of *paupertas viduae* would form the just cause required by canon law in such instances.[125] It is the welfare of the children that is of first consideration, together with the probability of incontinency on the part of the widow. If such circumstances can be successfully dealt with by means of a mixed or disparate marriage, there seems to be no good reason for insisting that the cause should apply only to the impediments of consanguinity or affinity.

6. The Advantage of Peace. (Bonum pacis)

By this term are signified not only the alliances between states and princes but also the cessation of serious private hatred, enmities and quarrels. This cause is invoked for extinguishing grave hostilities which have arisen between the relatives of the contracting parties and which can be entirely settled by the celebration of marriage. It can also be invoked when grave hostilities have flourished among the relatives and, while peace has been restored, the celebration of marriage would be conducive in making the peace more lasting.[126]

It can easily be seen why the Church would be willing to grant a matrimonial dispensation that peace might be brought about between two states or between two reigning families because a state of unrest in such quarters would do violence to the common good. It is interesting to note, however, that she is no less anxious to restore or insure peace to private warring factions. The cause *pro bono pacis* as outlined in the Instruction [127] is intended to bring about a dispensation either for the purpose of restoring peace to certain factions or for giving permanence to a peace that has but recently been restored.

[125] *Cf.* Canon 1061.

[126] S. C. P. F., Instruction, 9 May, 1877, n. 6—*Collect, P. F.*, n. 1470.

[127] S. C. P. F., Instruction, 9 May, 1877, n. 6—*Collect, P. F.*, n. 1470.

The cause is to be invoked in the first instance when it so happens that the relatives of a prospective husband and wife are embroiled in quarrels or enmities. The man and woman are laboring under an impediment to their marriage. From the phrasing of the Instruction it is to be inferred that the impediments to be considered are those arising from consanguinity or affinity. If a dispensation is granted it can be seen that the relatives will settle into a peaceful mode of living.

In the second instance a basis for the cause *pro bono pacis* can be found in the fact that previously a hatred had existed between the relatives of the impeded man and woman but peace has been recently restored. The marriage between the man and woman is deemed necessary to assure permanence to the peace so lately effected.

In the sense outlined in the Instruction this cause *pro bono pacis* can resolve itself into:

a. The cause *propter inimicitias* if *de facto* grave hostility exists between relatives of the contracting parties.

b. *Pro confirmatione pacis* if peace has been but lately restored and can be confirmed through a marriage contract.

c. *Propter lites* when the settlement of a lawsuit raging between the parties themselves or between their relatives can be closed through marriage.[128]

The gravity of the hostility on which the cause *pro bono pacis* is invoked is to be determined through the prudent judgment of the one dispensing.[129] He can determine his judgment on the circumstances and quality of the things and persons involved and on the cause which gave rise to the hostility. Regularly, however, those enmities are regarded grave which arise from a severe or dreadful injury or from causes involving money matters.[130] Moreover for invoking the cause on this score it is not sufficient that the grave hostilities are feared or threatened but it is necessary that *de facto* they are a reality.[131] It sometimes happens, however, that a dispensation

[128] *Cf.* Gasparri, *De Matrimonio,* n. 308, note 2.

[129] Bangen, *De Sponsalibus,* p. 185; Vlaming, *Praelectiones Juris Matrimonii,* II, n. 428, 2.

[130] *Cf.* Schmalzgrueber, *Jus Ecclesiasticum Universum,* L. IV, tit. 16, n. 107.

[131] *Cf.* Bangen, *De Sponsalibus,* p. 185.

is given with this cause for *preventing* hostilities or lawsuits from taking place.[132]

Practical Application

In times past there is no doubt but that the canonical cause *pro bono pacis* was of practical value. When communities pursued a more individualized existence it was less difficult to disrupt good order and hence it was more necessary that peace should be jealously guarded. By this it is not to be implied that peace is a less acceptable virtue today than in the past but it seems as though the modern community would not have to resort so frequently to the use of a marriage contract to smooth the difficulties of two opposing factions. It should not be inferred, however, that the cause *pro bono pacis* could not be invoked advantageously in these days. It could so happen that enmity was so rife between opposing factions that the only hope of a peaceful settlement would lie in the granting of the matrimonial dispensation for which petition was being made. If the families involved are honest and upright and not ordinarily given to fighting and quarreling and if the hostilities are of a grave nature the cause *pro bono pacis* is a *gravis causa* and suffices even for the closer degrees of consanguinity and affinity.[133]

While the authors, whenever the cause *pro bono pacis* is treated, mention its value in dispensing from the impediments of consanguinity and affinity, there is nothing in the phrasing of the cause in the Instruction[134] that would exclude the possibility of using the cause, at least impulsively, in petitioning for dispensation from any other ecclesiastical impediment. In the first place the Instruction says that the cause is meant not only for the extinction of hostilities between states and princes but also for settling or averting quarrels between citizens. While very frequently the reigning families of two nations between whom enmities exist are related by consanguinity or affinity, it can just as frequently happen that hostilities can arise among them even though they are not related. Just as frequently too, it can happen that their differences can be settled by a marriage

132 Chelodi, *Jus Matrimoniale*, n. 46.

133 Payen, *De Matrimonio*, I, n. 745; Feije, *De Impedimentis*, n. 662; Vlaming, *Praelectiones Juris Matrimonii*, II, n. 428d.

134 S. C. P. F., Instruction, 9 May, 1877, n. 6—*Collect. P. F.*, n. 1470.

whether the two families are related or not. Hence in saying that the cause is designed to settle the difficulties between two states by permitting a marriage to take place between the reigning families, it is not to be inferred that a dispensation is required from the impediments of consanguinity or affinity. It could happen that the contracting parties were laboring under another impediment.

Since the cause is extended in use from the enmities between the heads of nations to the hostilities that could arise between private citizens, the same course of reasoning can be followed. In practice it more frequently happens that feuds arise between families that are related to each other rather than between unrelated ones. But it could happen that in a particular locality the family of a Catholic woman is locked in bitter contest with the family of the non-Catholic man. If a marriage between these two parties, who are impeded by the impediment of mixed religion or disparity of cult and not by the impediments of consanguinity and affinity, can bring peace to the warring factions, it would seem that the cause *pro bono pacis* can be invoked.

But the practical value of the cause *pro bono pacis* is questionable in these times especially among individual groups of citizens, with the possible exceptions of use being made of the cause for the impediments of consanguinity and affinity. Furthermore the advisability of permitting the cause to be regarded as more than an impulsive cause in dispensing from the impediments of mixed religion or disparity of cult is dangerous. It would be asking too much to grant a dispensation from the impediments of mixed religion or disparity of cult on the sole plea that such a marriage would avert hatred or assure continued peace between two families. It would be more natural to believe that when the religious element of the situation was brought to the attention of the warring factions a more bitter struggle might ensue.

7. *Excessive Familiarity. (Nimia, suspecta, periculosa familiaritas)*

An excessive, suspected, dangerous familiarity and also a dwelling together under the same roof, which dwelling cannot easily be prevented,[135] can be regarded as a canonical cause.

[135] S. C. P. F., Instruction, 9 May, 1877, n. 7—*Collect. P. F.*, n. 1470.

According to the common opinion this cause is a *causa inhonesta.*[136] This cause can be invoked by the woman for seeking dispensation to marry a man who is bound by an impediment when between herself and the man there is or has been excessive or suspected or dangerous familiarity, and together with this it may happen that they are living in the same house.[137]

This cause distinctly differs from another canonical cause, namely *infamia mulieris.* For invoking the cause of dangerous familiarity the familiarity need not be so dangerous and excessive as to involve the loss of the woman's reputation,[138] that is, so grave that the woman is already suspected of *copula illicita.* It need only be *simpliciter periculosa.*[139] Hence any familiarity existing between the man and the woman which is excessive, that is, exceeding the customary bounds of decorum, or suspected, that is, which could give rise to the suspicion that *copula illicita* has been had, or dangerous, that is, presenting an occasion for sin, can afford a basis for seeking a dispensation on the grounds of familiarity. The familiarity is further aggravated when the parties are living in the same house. In being willing to grant a dispensation when the conditions are verified the Church acts to avoid the scandal that would arise when the familiarity has actually given way to sin and to remove the occasion of sin which the dangerous familiarity is affording.[140] Unless something is done to remedy the existing condition there is a probable future danger that the woman will become defamed and will be forced to remain unmarried or be forced to marry unequally.[141] In this sense, this cause is, as it were, *infamia mulieris ante factum.* But more logically the cause concerns itself not so much with the infamy of the woman as with the danger of sin which the familiarity is causing. Hence the cause can be in-

136 Payen, *De Matrimonio,* I, n. 747.

137 "Nimia familiaritas ea est quae modum honestum excedit, suspecta vero, quae suspicionem ingerit inhonestae conversationis . . . citra copulam tamen; periculosa, quae proximam peccandi occasionem affert." Ballerini-Palmieri, 6, n. 1368 apud Payen, *De Matrimonio,* I, n. 747.

138 Contra Cappello, *De Sacramentis,* III, n. 266; Ballerini-Palmieri, n. 1368, apud Payen, *De Matrimonio,* I, n. 747.

139 Vlaming, *Praelectiones Juris Matrimonii,* II, n. 429.

140 Chelodi, *Jus Matrimoniale,* n. 46.

141 Payen, *De Matrimonio,* I, n. 747.

voked provided the familiarity, even secretly, is such that there is the danger of sin now or that there will be in the future; for example, if the woman must marry another man, there may be the probable danger of her carrying on illicit relations with the man she was denied the permission of marrying.[142]

In regard to the condition placed by the words: "Cohabitation under the same roof, which cannot easily be prevented," it can be said that the cohabitation can aggravate the already existing excessive, suspected and dangerous familiarity [143] or it could possibly be a motive itself for granting the dispensation sought. When the parties live in the same house and this condition cannot easily be averted, it is possible to invoke the cause of familiarity even if their cohabitation has not yet given rise to suspicion.[144]

Practical Application

There seems to be an agreement among the authors that regularly the cause of excessive familiarity does not of itself suffice for obtaining dispensation in the closer degrees of consanguinity and affinity. In the more remote degrees, however, it will be sufficient when through particular circumstances surrounding a particular case, more weight is given to the cause.[145] A particular circumstance which might aggravate a case could be the fear of a civil marriage. In such an instance this cause together with the cause of excessive familiarity could bring about a dispensation from consanguinity in the second degree.[146]

In general then it might be said that the cause of excessive familiarity, while it is a canonical cause, is none the less, simply an impulsive cause. The authors, too, in treating it briefly as they do, concern themselves only with the possibility of it being applied to the impediments of consanguinity and affinity. There is nothing in the

[142] Vlaming, *Praelectiones Juris Matrimonii,* II, n. 429.

[143] Rosset, *De Sacramento Matrimonii,* 4, n. 2586, apud Payen, *De Matrimonio,* I, n. 747.

[144] *Cf.* Payen, *De Matrimonio,* I, n. 747.

[145] *Cf.* Feije *De Impedimentis,* n. 674; Giovine, *De Dispensationibus Matrimonialibus,* I, p. 378.

[146] Payen, *De Matrimonio,* I, n. 747.

phrasing of the Instruction that would imply such a limitation. Nor is there any reason for believing that excessive familiarity would exist only between relatives. Hence if the cause is admitted at all, it should be admitted, at least impulsively, for any ecclesiastical impediment to which, by nature, it could be applied. As to its practical value, however, little can be said. It seems reasonable to follow Vlaming,[147] in holding that conditions for verifying the cause of excessive familiarity as herein explained will seldom exist. Usually when a courtship has progressed to the stage when a dispensation is sought and when it has been carried on under the conditions which ordinarily suffice for the cause of excessive familiarity, very often *diffamatio mulieris* can in truth be alleged rather than excessive familiarity. In other words it seems that the conditions on which the cause of excessive familiarity are based are so delicately distinct from the cause of *diffamatio mulieris* that when they are perfectly fulfilled, that is, complied with so that their use in actual practice can be applied, the condition of *diffamatio mulieris* actually exists.

8. *Copula Jam Habita*

"Copula cum consanguinea vel affini, vel alia persona impedimento laborante, praehabita, et praegnantia, ideoque, legitimatio prolis, ut nempe consulatur bono prolis ipsius, et honori mulieris, quae secus innupta maneret. Haec profecto una est ex urgentioribus causis, ob quam etiam plebeis dari solet dispensatio dummodo copula patrata non fuerit sub spe facilioris dispensationis; quae circumstantia in supplicatione foret exprimeda." [147a]

From the words in which the conditions for the cause are expressed it can be seen that this cause is regarded as one of the more urgent causes through which matrimonial dispensations may be obtained. In curial practice this cause is expressed in various terms, namely, *"infamia cum copula," "cum copula scienter"* or *"ob scandala vitanda."*[148]

That the conditions for pleading the cause may be verified it is only necessary that *copula* has been had between two persons who

[147] Vlaming, *Praelectiones Juris Matrimonii,* II, n. 429.

[147a] S. C. P. F., Instruction, 9 May, 1877, n. 8.—*Collect. P. F.*, n. 1470.

[148] Feije, *De Impedimentis,* n. 675.

are bound by the impediments of consanguinity or affinity or by any other impediment. If *praegnantia subsequens* can also be alleged, the cause of *copula jam habita* is so much the more strengthened for then the *legitimatio prolis* must be a consideration. But strictly speaking only *copula* suffices for seeking the dispensation.[149]

According to the general opinion for the cause to be perfectly verified it is necessary that the *copula* which has already taken place is a known fact or that its existence will soon become a known fact.[150]

The present or impending notoriety will be the source of the woman's loss of reputation and consequent difficulty of finding a husband and it is these two evils that the Church is desirous of averting in admiting the use of the cause. The authors, however, who admit the desirability of the conditions for the cause being perfectly fulfilled, are by no means adverse to the cause being invoked when *copula secreta sine praegnantia* is had. In this instance, since the act is not public and the disgrace of the woman is not threatened, the dispensation is granted that danger of incontinence may be removed.[151] Discretion, however, must be used in invoking the cause on the grounds of *copula occulta*. Neither danger nor embarrassment is ordinarily incurred when the dispensation is petitioned in the internal forum. When it is sought in the external forum, however, the cause of *copula secreta* should not be expressed except with the consent of the petitioners and only with great prudence.[152]

Prudence will dictate that if the cause of *copula* is *per se* a most urgent one, the fact of *praegnantia subsequens* will render the cause even more grave. In fact, the cause could then be classified as *causa urgentissima,* even though the *praegnantia* is occult and will remain so.[153] A dispensation granted on the grounds of pregnancy brings about a twofold favor. In the one instance, that the woman's repu-

[149] Payen, *De Matrimonio,* I, n. 748.

[150] De Smet, *Betrothment and Marriage,* II, n. 823; Payen, *De Matrimonio,* I, n. 748; Feije, *De Impedimentis,* n. 675; Vlaming, *Praelectiones Juris Matrimonii,* II, n. 430.

[151] Genicot-Salsmanns, *Institutiones Theologiae Moralis,* II, n. 525; Feije, *De Impedimentis,* n. 675; Vlaming, *Praelectiones Juris Matrimonii,* II, n. 430.

[152] Cappello, *De Sacramentis,* III, n. 266.

[153] Payen, *De Matrimonio,* I, n. 748.

tation may be completely saved or at least not entirely ruined; in the other instance, that the child born may be born legitimate or if already born, it may be rendered legitimate through subsequent marriage provided Canon 1116 can be invoked. Furthermore, the granting of a dispensation *propter praegnantiam* will make for the public welfare through the lessening of scandal.[154]

In placing the conditions necessary for verifying the use of the cause the Propaganda notes: "This cause is one of the most urgent, and, on account of it, it is customary to grant a dispensation even to those of the lowest class provided they have not so acted for the purpose of obtaining a dispensation more easily; should this be the case it would have to be mentioned in the petition." According to former interpretation if *copula* was had for the purpose of more easily obtaining the dispensation sought and no mention was made of the fraud in the petition for dispensation, the dispensation was invalid. The Sacred Congregation of the Holy Office, however, in two responses [155] decreed that it was not necessary for the validity or liceity of the dispensation to mention such fraud.

Practical Application

From the sense of the words in which the Propaganda expresses this cause, the practical value of the cause cannot be questioned. In her desire to save the woman's reputation, to render the child legitimate and to assure the public good of the state, the Church is willing to admit the cause even in favor of those who come of less distinguished families. The cause is of such weight that it is readily admitted for dispensing from the graver impediments, for instance, from the second degree of consanguinity or from the first degree of affinity in the collateral line.[156]

In the application of this cause there need be no doubt as to its extent. The Propaganda very clearly states that it can be invoked in favor of persons bound by the impediments of consanguinity or

[154] Payen, *De Matrimonio,* I, n. 748; De Smet, *Betrothment and Marriage,* II, n. 823, note 8; Feije, *De Impedimentis,* n. 675.

[155] S. C. S. Off., 25 June, 1885—*Collect. P. F.*, n. 1635; 18 March, 1891—*Collect, P. F.*, n. 1749.

[156] Payen, *De Matrimonio,* I, n. 748.

affinity or by any other impediment. *"Copula cum consanguinea vel affini vel alia persona impedimento laborante praehabita."* Surely from the words of the cause it can be inferred that its use can be invoked for dispensing from any of the impediments, *servatis servandis,* which the Church regards as dispensable. It should be borne in mind, however, that for invoking the cause in petitioning for dispensation in *foro externo,* discretion and prudence should be used. While the cause is a grave one and its use most effective, particularly when *praegnantia subsequens* is present, there is the danger that its invocation may redound unfavorably to the reputation of those involved. Prudence and charity will dictate that if possible, an equally weighty and more honest cause should be used for petitioning in *foro externo.* If, however, *copula jam habita* is the only cause that can be invoked and sufficient minor causes are lacking to form an aggregate final cause, the only alternative lies in using this grave and disparaging cause. The use of the cause will not redound so unfavorably to the reputation of those involved as will the denial of the dispensation because of the unwillingness to make use of such a disparaging cause.

9. Evil Repute of the Woman. (Copulae suspicio)

"Infamia mulieris, ex suspicione orta quod illa, suo consanguineo aut affini nimis familiaris, cognita sit ab eodem, licet suspicio sit falsa; cum nempe, nisi matrimonium contrahatur, vel innupta remaneret, vel disparis condicionis viro nubere deberet, aut gravia damna orirentur." [157]

Authorities are in agreement as to the disparaging character of this cause.[158] The reason for admitting this cause lies in the fact that the woman is suspected, although falsely of *copula.* The suspicion arises from the fact that excessive familiarity existed between the woman and the relative she is desirous of marrying. The suspicion is of such a nature that, while it may rest on a false basis, it has caused the woman to be gravely defamed in the estimation of the people.

[157] S. C. P. F., *Instruction,* 9 May, 1877, n. 9—*Collect. P. F.,* n. 1470.

[158] *Cf.* Payen, *De Matrimonio,* I, n. 749; Vromant, *Facultates Apostolicae,* n. 61; Farrugia, *De Matrimonio,* n. 98.

The cause is admitted in use on the plea that the petitioner, being a disgraced woman, will be forced to remain unmarried, or be forced to marry beneath her station or be exposed to serious loss. While the *diffamatio* is to be of such a nature that the woman is faced with the probability of remaining unmarried or of marrying unequally, it is not necessary in invoking the cause to determine minutely the presence of this danger. It has been aptly remarked: *ubi enim mulieris fama semel laesa est, ibi praedictum periculum, generatim loquendo, per se adest.*[159] This cause can be invoked only for removing the impediments of consanguinity and affinity.[160]

Practical Application

There can be little doubt as to the practical value of this cause. It is a *causa gravis* and to all intents and purposes is almost as effective a cause as is *copula jam habita cum praegnantia desit.* In fact there is much similarity in the three disparaging causes of *nimia suspecta, copula jam habita* and *copulae suspicio.* In verifying the exact conditions of their application minute differences are to be found. All three, however, are designed for the same purpose, namely, the safeguarding of the woman's reputation and the removal of scandal.[161]

10. Revalidation of an Invalid Marriage. (Revalidatio Matrimonii Invalidi)

The revalidation of a marriage contracted in good faith and publicly, according to the canonical form. A dissolution of a marriage of this nature could scarcely take place without causing public scandal and grave injury, especially to the woman,[162] but if the parties have contracted in bad faith, they do not in any way deserve the favor of a dispensation, as the Council of Trent has decreed.[163]

159 *Nouvelle Revue Theologique,* X, p. 33.

160 *Cf.* Vromant, *Jus Missionariorum,* V. *De Matrimonio,* n. 152.

161 *Cf.* Payen, *De Matrimonio,* I, n. 749.

162 Cap. 7, *De Consanguin.*

163 Conc. Trident., sess., XXIV, *De ref matrim.,* c. 5. "Si quis intra gradus prohibitos scienter matrimonium contrahere praesumpserit, separetur, et spe dispensationis obtinendae careat . . . "

This cause is, naturally, one of the principal causes on which a matrimonial dispensation can be based. For invoking it the invalidity of the marriage is presupposed. Since the marriage involved is invalid, the law demands that the contractants dissolve their invalid contract. It is at this point that the canonical cause of the revalidation of an invalid marriage is invoked. It is to be inferred from the words of the Propaganda,[164] that the Church in her solicitude for the welfare of souls is willing to revalidate the marriage. If she adhered to the letter of the law and insisted on the dissolution of the marriage, she is aware that such a dissolution would almost invariably cause grave public scandal, or even if this could be avoided, the parties and especially the woman, and children if there be any, would be made to suffer grave harm.

In former times the cause of *revalidatio* could be applied without question only to a marriage that had been contracted in good faith on the part of both or at least on the part of one of the parties. That is, the marriage would be contracted and only afterward would the invalidity be discovered. If both parties were in bad faith and contracted the marriage while being aware of the invalidating impediment, the cause could be invoked but the fraud of the parties would render it more difficult to obtain the dispensation sought or might even cause the dispensation to be denied.[165]

Under the present discipline, however, a dispensation for the cause of revalidation would not be refused to those who had contracted in bad faith.[166] This is especially true if children are already born of the union,[167] or if the marriage was contracted civilly or *coram ministello*. The fact that children have been born of the marriage for which dispensation is being sought adds to the gravity of the cause for if the union were ordered to be dissolved, it would be the children who would suffer. The fact that the marriage may have been contracted civilly or *coram ministello* prompts the one dispensing to authorize its revalidation that the scandal already caused might be repaired and that the Catholic party, if it is a case

[164] S. C. P. F., Instruction, 9 May, 1877, n. 10—*Collect. P. F.*, n. 1470.

[165] *Cf.* De Smet, *Betrothment and Marriage*, II, n. 824.

[166] Wernz, *Jus Decretalium*, I, n. 630, note 158.

[167] De Smet, *Betrothment and Marriage*, II, n. 824.

of a mixed marriage, might be removed from the danger of living outside the Church altogether.[168] When this cause then was proposed by the Propaganda the title for it was correctly fixed in the words: "the revalidation of a marriage that has been contracted in good faith and publicly, according to the canonical form." While these words properly imply the revalidation of an invalid marriage, their use was restricted to a marriage which was invalid not through lack of form but because an invalidating impediment was discovered after the marriage had been contracted. The parties, or at least one of them, were entirely ignorant of the existing impediment. At the present time, however, it seems that this cause may be expressed in the words: "the revalidation of an invalid marriage." The revalidation can be applied to any marriage already contracted (provided the Church is accustomed to dispense from the impediment involved). Marriage is considered contracted when it is celebrated in such a manner that it bears the form or appearance of marriage; civil marriage of persons subject to the law of clandestinity, and marriage celebrated before an heretical minister can be considered as contracted marriages and as such are capable of revalidation and even of *sanatio in radice,* provided that it is certain that the parties had the intention of eliciting the real matrimonial consent,[169] whether the marriage is null because of lack of form or because of some diriment impediment, regardless of the good or bad faith of the contractants.[170]

In extending the use of this cause to embrace unions contracted in bad faith and contrary to the canonical form, the Holy See declares that the circumstances surrounding the marriage to be convalidated must be mentioned. For instance, it must be mentioned whether the marriage was contracted in good faith (at least by one of the parties) or whether it was contracted with knowledge of the impediment; or if the banns have been published [171] and the canonical form observed [172] whether the marriage has been contracted in the hope of obtaining a dispensation more easily or whether it has been

[168] *Cf.* Gasparri, *De Matrimonio,* n. 312, note 2.
[169] *Cf.* De Smet, *Betrothment and Marriage,* II, n. 733.
[170] Chelodi, *Jus Matrimoniale,* n. 46.
[171] Canon 1022.
[172] Canon 1094.

already consummated.[173] The above conditions need be noted only when the marriage involved was contracted in the Church. Such a marriage was possible because of fraud at least on the part of one of the contractants. The conditions surrounding a marriage that was only civilly contracted need not be stressed.[174]

Practical Application

There can be no doubt of the practical value of the cause of *revalidatio matrimonii invalidi.* It is a cause that is frequently invoked and furthermore it is ranked among the "more grave" causes.[175] For this reason it alone suffices for petitioning dispensation from any of the ecclesiastical impediments, even the graver ones, from which the Church is accustomed to grant dispensation.[176] In this country, in particular, the cause of revalidation comes frequently into practice, especially for revalidating marriages that have been contracted civilly or *coram ministello.* It so happens that two contracting parties, one of whom usually is a non-Catholic, being denied ecclesiastical sanction to their proposed marriage or often without even seeking this sanction, contract civilly or *coram ministello.* If the union continues the Catholic party is living in sin and this is a source of scandal to all who are aware of the facts of the case. In such an instance, if the cause of *revalidatio* is not admitted, the scandal will continue, and the Catholic party, together with the children who may be born of the union, will be exposed to the constant danger of apostatizing from the Catholic faith. The Church in her solicitude for souls will do all in her power to avert such evils and hence admits *revalidatio* as a canonical cause.

11. Danger of a Mixed Marriage or of the Celebration of the Marriage Before a non-Catholic Minister. (Periculum matrimonii mixti vel coram ministello)

There is a just cause for dispensation when there is danger that those who wish to contract marriage, even in a near degree of rela-

[173] *Cf.* De Smet, *Betrothment and Marriage,* II, n. 848.

[174] *Cf.* Decision of S. Penitentiary, 8 April, 1831.

[175] *Cf.* Chelodi, *Jus Matrimoniale,* n. 46.

[176] *Cf.* Payen, *De Matrimonio,* I, n. 750.

tionship, will, in contempt of the Church's authority, contract before a non-Catholic minister, if the dispensation is denied. In such instances the dispensation is granted, not only because of the scandal that would be given to the faithful, but also because of the danger of perversion and apostacy of the contracting parties, especially in regions where heretics enjoy full liberty. Likewise the fear is present that if the dispensation is denied, one or both parties will eventually marry a non-Catholic.[177]

This cause as stated by the Propaganda is extended to two different circumstances. In one instance there is to be considered the possibility and grave danger of two Catholics contracting before a non-Catholic minister if they are denied dispensation from the impediment which makes their marriage an impossibility in the Church. In the other instance there is to be considered the possibility or danger that one or both Catholics, on being denied the dispensation will abandon the idea of contracting marriage between themselves and will finally marry some non-Catholic.

In practice it is the first case, namely, where the two Catholics will go before a minister, that will more often have to be considered. When two persons have the desire to marry each other, on being denied a dispensation, they are liable to contract marriage regardless of ecclesiastical authority rather than give each other up and eventually marry some one else. In general such will be the result in those places where mixed marriages are more common. In Holland, particularly, however, and in some other parts of Europe, the percentage of mixed marriages has been reduced to a minimum due to the fact that ecclesiastical authorities in these countries have taken a firm stand against the granting of dispensations for mixed religion and disparity of cult. Naturally in these countries it cannot be said that the refusal of a dispensation will consequently result in marriage outside the Church. More frequently the parties concerned will accept the decision of the Church and will abandon the idea of attempting marriage civilly or *coram ministello*.[178]

For the application of the cause, however, either case can be present, namely, either the danger of a mixed marriage or the dan-

[177] S. C. P. F., Instruction, 9 May, 1877, n. 11—*Collect. P. F.*, n. 1470.

[178] *Cf.* Ter Haar-Connell, *Mixed Marriages and Their Remedies*, n. 139.

ger of two Catholics contracting before a non-Catholic minister. In short it is only necessary that the element of *danger* is present and the cause will be verified according to the gravity of the danger.

In former times, *i. e.*, shortly following the Reformation, it is known that the cause of a mixed marriage or *coram ministello* (known as *periculum fidei*) was easily admitted for removing an impediment existing between two Catholics. This apparent leniency was due to the fact that in some regions, especially in Germany and Belgium, it was often difficult to determine the exact religious views of the people. It could happen in those days that a marriage could be contracted and only afterward would it be discovered that one of the contractants fostered decidedly heretical beliefs. Often such a union would cause the truly Catholic party to apostatize. The danger then of a mixed marriage or of a marriage *coram ministello* was always present and its existence was admitted, as it were, *in globo*.[179]

In these times, however, since heretics are known and are separated from Catholics their mere presence does not at once constitute a right to invoke the canonical cause of mixed marriage or *coram ministello*. The danger is no longer *in globo* but rather *in individuo*. Before invoking the cause it must be established that in each individual case the danger is really present so that the Catholic parties, on being denied the petitioned dispensation, will contract marriage with a non-Catholic, either baptized or not, or will go themselves before a non-Catholic minister and marry.[180]

The right to invoke the cause, then, will depend on the true and individual danger present in each case. It should not be said, perhaps, that the danger of mixed marriages or of marriages *coram ministello* is less prevalent today than in former times but curial practice has ruled that the danger in general is not so great. In each individual case it must be established that danger exists.

Nor is it established that danger of a mixed marriage or of marriage *coram ministello* exists when the parties involved threaten that they will turn from the faith if the dispensation which they seek is denied.[181] The mere threat is not sufficient, nor is an actual threat

[179] *Cf.* Feije, *De Impedimentis*, n. 666.

[180] *Cf.* Payen, *De Matrimonio*, I, n. 751.

[181] *Cf.* Feije, *De Impedimentis*, n. 666.

necessary. If, however, there is strong probability that the parties will carry out the threat, the reason for invoking the cause becomes more necessary. The one dispensing can determine the probability of danger from the disposition of the parties seeking the dispensation. If on previous occasions, they have shown themselves to be weak in the faith, or if they belong to families marked for their indifference toward Catholicism, then, practically speaking, a probable danger of a mixed marriage or of a marriage *coram ministello* exists.[182]

The danger, then, required for invoking this cause can arise from a twofold source: the common danger arising from the number of heretics and the number of mixed marriages existing in a particular locality; and the danger arising from the wilful disposition or the indifferentism of the petitioners. Ordinarily the common danger arising from the large number of heretics living in a certain locality will make the cause only impulsive.[183] As an impulsive cause it can be admitted in the closer degrees of consanguinity and affinity provided other, though less grave causes, are also present.[184]

When the danger of a mixed marriage or of a marriage *coram ministello* arises from the perverted will of the petitioners and it has been determined, through circumstances surrounding the case, that the danger is probable, then the cause can be a final cause and can be admitted even in the closer degrees, for instance in the first degree of affinity in the collateral line.[185]

Practical Application

If the strict wording of the Instruction of the Propaganda is adhered to, the practical value of this cause is questionable. In the first place, the danger of a mixed marriage as implied in the Instruction will rarely be present. As has been remarked it will not often happen that two Catholics, on being denied a dispensation, will break their engagement, and sometime afterward will contract with a heretic. The danger of marriage before a non-Catholic minister, however, is more prevalent, and this is a circumstance that has to be

[182] Vlaming, *Praelectiones Juris Matrimoni,* II, n. 433.

[183] Vlaming, *Praelectiones Juris Matrimonii,* II, n. 433.

[184] *Cf.* Bangen, *De Sponsalibus et Matrimonio,* II, p. 189.

[185] *Cf.* Bangen, *De Sponsalibus et Matrimonio,* II, p. 196.

too frequently contended with especially in America. But even then, to make this angle of the cause of practical value in America, it must be extended so as to embrace the impediments of mixed religion and disparity of cult. It is true that when this is the case, the mixed marriage, which the cause wishes to avert is present. Nevertheless, the Church in America is faced with two alternatives: a Catholic and a non-Catholic wish to contract marriage; since they are determined to marry, if the dispensation is refused the parties will be strongly tempted to contract before a civil magistrate or an heretical minister. If they adopt this latter course the marriage will not only have been contracted outside the Church but the Catholic party will also have incurred an excommunication.[186] This, naturally, will be a further evil that the Church wishes to avoid. Too often when marriages are contracted outside the Church the Catholic party is lost to the Faith. On the other hand, if the Church grants the dispensation for the mixed or disparate marriage, the marriage will take place in the Church and there will be some hope that the Catholic party may persevere in the Faith or may even convert the non-Catholic party.

To restrict this cause to the impediments of consanguinity and affinity will make the cause impractical in America. Because of local conditions and customs it is almost certain that Catholics and non-Catholics will contract marriage among themselves. If dispensation will not be granted to them it oftentimes happens that they will contract outside the Church. If the cause is to be admitted for the impediments of mixed religion and disparity of cult, it can be invoked only when the danger of marriage *coram ministello* is really present.[187] The presence of a large number of heretics in a community or the fact that many marriages have already been contracted *coram ministello* need not *per se* verify the conditions for invoking the cause.[188] But if the pastor in his prudent judgment, even without questioning the parties, believes that the faith of the Catholic party is weak and that he can easily be persuaded by the non-Catholic party to marry outside the Church or that the Catholic party

[186] *Cf.* Canon 2319, § 1, n. 1.

[187] *Cf.* Payen, *De Matrimonio*, I, n. 751.

[188] *Cf.* Vlaming, *Praelectiones Juris Matrimonii*, II, n. 433; Bangen, *De Sponsalibus et Matrimonio*, II, p. 189; Feije, *De Impedimentis*, n. 666.

is of so headstrong a disposition as to determine to marry regardless of the consequences, these facts together with the fact that a strong non-Catholic atmosphere dominates the locality, will justify invoking the canonical cause of danger of contracting *coram ministello.*

It has been objected that when the danger of marriage before a civil magistrate or an heretical minister exists the *cautiones* required and given prior to marriage cannot be sincere.[189] This might be true in specific instances or in particular localities but there is no reason for believing that suspicion of insincerity arises in every such case. When the non-Catholic party signs the *cautiones* he does so because the Church requires him to and up to and including the signing of the *cautiones* he has signified his willingness to do all that the Church asks him to do. Objectively, there is no reason to doubt his sincerity. It is only when he learns that the Church will not go further and permit his Catholic marriage that he (and the Catholic party with him) threatens to marry outside the Church. Hence, as Schenk ably notes,[190] the foundation of the cause of danger of marriage outside the Church rests more often on the determination to marry rather than on the insincerity of the parties in signing the promises.

12. Danger of Incestuous Concubinage. (Periculum incestuosi concubinatus)

The words used by the Propaganda [191] in stating this canonical cause are quite evident in themselves. The concubinage which the Church wishes to avert in this instance is that which would arise among relatives if the matrimonial dispensation which they are petitioning is denied. In admitting the use of the cause the Church wishes to avert the scandal which would arise from such an evil. Furthermore, the Church is aware that if the parties involved would actually fall into the practice they would jeopardize their eternal salvation.

[189] *Cf.* Vlaming, *Praelectiones Juris Matrimonii,* II, n. 217.

[190] *Cf.* Schenk, *The Matrimonial Impediment of Mixed Religion and Disparity of Cult,* n. 291.

[191] *Cf.* S. C. P. F., Instruction, 9 May, 1877—(*Collect. P. F.*, n. 1470.

This canonical cause can be invoked if it is established that the denial of a matrimonial dispensation to two relatives will constitute the danger of their assuming a state of concubinage. A probable danger will be sufficient grounds for invoking the cause.[192]

In a given instance this cause can be a just one even in the closer degrees of consanguinity and affinity, for example, in the second degree of affinity, provided that the danger is real. If it can be judged from the temperament and circumstances of the parties involved that they would not hesitate to practice incestuous concubinage if the dispensation is denied, then the danger of such an evil exists and the canonical cause can be invoked.[193]

Practical Application

Under local conditions consanguineous marriages are quite the exception. Hence this canonical cause will be of little practical value. If in a given case, conditions for verifying it should arise, the circumstances of the case would have to be considered. In practice, however, it would seem that when a dispensation is denied, the danger of a civil marriage or of a marriage *coram ministello* will more often threaten than will the danger of an incestuous concubinage.

13. Danger of a Civil Marriage. (Periculum matrimonii civilis)

This canonical cause is verified when there is probable danger that persons, seeking a dispensation and not obtaining it, will contract a purely civil marriage.[194]

It is quite evident that this canonical cause is not unlike the two preceding causes listed by the Propaganda, namely, danger of marriage *coram ministello* and danger of incestuous concubinage. In each of the three causes the element of danger is present. They differ from each other only in as much as the element of danger in each cause threatens a different evil. Because of the similarity of this cause with the other two, there must exist at least a probable danger

[192] *Cf.* Payen, *De Matrimonio,* I, n. 752.

[193] *Cf.* Payen, *De Matrimonio,* I, n. 752.

[194] S. C. P. F., Instruction, 9 May, 1877, n. 13—*Collect. P. F.,* n. 1470.

that the parties involved will contract a civil marriage if the dispensation which they are seeking is denied.[195] Hence, the mere threat of the parties to contract civilly upon refusal of the dispensation will not be sufficient grounds for invoking the cause.[196] Prudence must be used in this regard lest, by granting dispensation on slight provocation or from the mere threats of the parties, a formal contempt of the Church will be brought about. Such a practice would also beget religious indifference.[197]

If, however, the pastor, through whom the dispensation is being sought, has a probable fear that the parties will contract civilly if the dispensation is denied, he can petition dispensation on the grounds of this cause. Furthermore, he can arrive at this probable fear even though the parties involved have not by an express declaration threatened to contract the marriage civilly. If the pastor is acquainted with the temperament of the locality in which the parties live and if he knows that in the past parties similarly situated have not hesitated to contract civilly, it would seem that his fear is well founded that the parties now seeking dispensation would not hesitate to follow the established practice.

Furthermore, for determining the probability of a civil marriage in a given case the element of time can be a consideration. For instance, two parties laboring under the impediment of disparity of cult present themselves before a priest for marriage. Ordinarily such an impediment is not dispensed from except after the lapse of a considerable length of time during which the non-Catholic party undergoes a course of instruction. If, however, the parties in question, because they are about to embark upon a journey and for this reason will not delay until the dispensation is granted through the routine channels, are determined to contract marriage civilly, it can be held that the danger of their contracting a civil marriage is really present.

When the Church grants a dispensation for the cause of danger

[195] *Cf.* Payen, *De Matrimonio,* I, n. 753.

[196] *Cf.* De Smet, *Betrothment and Marriage,* II, n. 826; Vlaming, *Praelectiones Juris Matrimonii,* II, n. 435.

[197] *Cf.* Genicot-Salsmanns, *Institutiones Theologiae Moralis,* II, n. 525; Vermeersch-Creusen, *Epitome Juris Canonici,* II, n. 318.

of a civil marriage she so acts that probable scandal might be averted and that the parties involved might be less subject to the risk of losing their souls.[198]

Practical Application

In those places in which Catholics are in the minority, there can be little doubt as to the practical value of this canonical cause. While *per se* the presence of heretics does not constitute a grave danger of a civil marriage or of a marriage *coram ministello,*[199] nevertheless, it cannot be denied that a strong non-Catholic sentiment pervading a community will oftentimes make indifferent Catholics more indifferent to the authority of the Church.

For all practical purposes there need be no distinction in America between the two canonical causes of danger of a marriage being contracted *coram ministello* and danger of a marriage being contracted civilly. Aside from the fact that in the one instance, namely, marriage *coram ministello,* the Catholic party incurs excommunication and in the other attempted marriage does not incur the excommunication, the fact remains that the marriage has been contracted *extra ecclesiam* and this is the evil that the Church must avert.

To cope with this evil it would seem that both these canonical causes should be admitted for the impediments of mixed religion and disparity of cult.[200] It may be objected that these causes are voluntary, depending on the will of the petitioners, and hence strictly speaking are insufficient.[201] It may further be objected that the use of these causes for the impediments of mixed religion and disparity of cult implies, as it were, a contradiction.[202] On entering the marriage, the parties to the contract sign *cautiones* that they hold in reverence the Church's doctrine on marriage and are willing to comply with whatever conditions the Church may impose. While the parties signify themselves so willing in this regard they are neverthe-

[198] *Cf.* Payen, *De Matrimonio*, I, nn. 752, 753.

[199] *Cf.* Vlaming, *Praelectiones Juris Matrimonii,* II, n. 433.

[200] *Cf.* Petrovits, *The New Church Law on Matrimony,* n. 245.

[201] *Cf.* Feije, *De Impedimentis,* n. 660.

[202] *Cf.* Vlaming, *Praelectiones Juris Matrimonii,* I, n. 217.

less determined to marry,[203] and if they are denied the right of marriage in the Church they will attempt marriage *extra ecclesiam.* It is in this attitude that the contradiction seems to lie. There is no denying the fact that the contractants show themselves to be of a perverse will and in such instances the Catholic party cannot be held blameless in practically forcing the hand of the Church.[204] In admitting these canonical causes for obtaining dispensation from the impediments of mixed religion or disparity of cult, the Church is simply choosing the lesser of two evils.[205]

It is a sad commentary on the Catholic Faith that these canonical causes have to be admitted but in these times it seems that the Church has no other alternative. When the parties to a mixed marriage show themselves determined to marry regardless of consequences, it might be urged that the Church should withdraw her interest from such self-willed and indifferent Catholics and permit them to pursue the folly of their ways. It would seem that this attitude on the part of the Church would be often wanting in wisdom. It is a well-known fact that sheep will follow the leader regardless of danger. It is the part of the wise shepherd to so direct the leader that the flock will be led in safety. The Church fills the rôle of the shepherd for her strong-willed subjects. If indifferent Catholics are prevailed upon by their prospective non-Catholic spouses to turn from the Church and contract civilly or *coram ministello,* it would seem that the Church would display wisdom in making a rather compromising move to attract the interest of the non-Catholic party and to grant the desired dispensation, but only when there is real danger that the parties will contract *extra ecclesiam.* In such a course of action the interest of the non-Catholic may be so aroused as to prompt him to embrace the Catholic Faith. If the dispensation is denied, when the parties are willing to sign the *cautiones,* the non-Catholic party will certainly be lost to the Faith and in all probability so will the Catholic party. Furthermore, when such invalid marriages are con-

[203] *Cf.* Schenk, *The Matrimonial Impediments of Mixed Religion and Disparity of Cult,* n. 291.

[204] *Cf.* De Becker, *De Sponsalibus et Matrimonio Praelectiones Canonicae,* p. 330.

[205] *Cf.* Payen, *De Matrimonio,* I, n. 864.

tracted, in order to revalidate them, if the parties are at all willing, the Church is prompted to act for the purpose of repairing the scandal and to legitimatize the children if there be any. In the final analysis, the revalidation is but a compromise move. There seems to be more reason for, and less danger in, such a move before the marriage has been contracted *extra ecclesiam* than afterwards for before the marriage the parties are willing to observe the form if the dispensation is granted and there is a reasonable assurance had that they will fulfill the conditions of the *cautiones*. After the marriage has been contracted *extra ecclesiam* in most instances both parties are lost to the Faith. The choice of the lesser of two evils lies in the Church's admitting the use of the canonical cause of danger of a civil marriage or of a marriage contracted *coram ministello* for the impediments of mixed religion and disparity of cult as often as a real danger threatens and as often as the danger cannot be averted in any other way.

14. The Removal of Grave Scandals. (Remotio gravium scandalorum)

The Propaganda simply states this cause without making further comment.[206]

Little need be said concerning this cause since the phrase through which it is expressed is sufficiently comprehensive. Prudence dictates that if a grave scandal can be averted or lessened through the concession of a dispensation this fact alone constitutes the reason for conceding the dispensation.

Under the name of scandals can be classified any cause, occasion or probable danger of grave sins. Hence any condition that fosters the occurrence or probable occurrence of *fornicatio vel concubinatus* or of grave hostilities or injuries or other circumstances of this nature can become the object of the canonical cause of the removal of grave scandal.[207]

For invoking this canonical cause it is only necessary to ascertain that a scandal already exists or that it probably will exist. The cause

[206] *Cf.* S. C. P. F., Instruction, 9 May, 1877, n. 14—*Collect. P. F.*, n. 1470.
[207] *Cf.* Vlaming, *Praelectiones Juris Matrimonii*, II, n. 436.

will be just provided that the marriage for which dispensation is sought will be efficacious in removing or averting the grave scandal. The graver the scandal the more urgent will be the cause.[208]

Practical Application

In practice it would seem that enumeration of this canonical cause is more or less superfluous. For the most part the so-called infamous causes,, *e. g., nimia familiaritas, copulae suspicio, periculum matrimonii mixti,* are invoked both for the purpose of removing the danger or occasion of sin from the petitioners and for the purpose of repairing or removing scandal. The canonical cause, for the sake of peace, can be considered in the same light, since when peace is brought about the scandals arising from enmities and injuries are repaired or removed.

It would seem, then, that the canonical cause of the removal of grave scandals should be invoked properly as an impulsive cause, or it can be invoked as a final cause when, because of its vagueness, it is more desirable that it should be used than any of the more specific and more glaring dishonest causes.

15. The Cessation of Notorious Concubinage. (Cessatio public concubinatus)

The words used by the Propaganda in expressing this canonical cause are sufficiently clear.[209] The cause can be invoked when the parties seeking dispensation are living in a state of notorious concubinage. By nature this cause is most grave for notorious concubinage is a source of scandal, it brings infamy on the parties involved, especially the woman, it works to the detriment of the children who are illegitimate and it places in jeopardy the souls of the persons involved.[210]

Practical Application

For the most part, unless the parties are living in common-law

[208] *Cf.* Payen, *De Matrimonio,* I, n. 754.

[209] *Cf.* S. C. P. F., Instruction, 9 May, 1877, n. 15—*Collect. P. F.,* n. 1470.

[210] *Cf.* Payen, *De Matrimonio,* I, n. 755.

marriage, incestuous concubinage will arise because they have not observed the canonical form of marriage.[211] In taking steps to convalidate such a marriage it seems proper in charity not to expressly call attention to the fact that a state of incestuous concubinage exists. Although in seeking dispensation from the impediments of consanguinity or affinity in order that a marriage might be convalidated, if the parties have been living together the presence of incestuous concubinage is implied. But the guilt of the parties does not become so evident if the canonical cause on which the dispensation is being sought is not expressly stated in the words: that the state of incestuous concubinage be removed. It would be better to apply for the convalidation making mention of the fact that the marriage of the parties involved is impeded because of consanguinity and affinity and further that the parties had already contracted, for example, civilly.[212] Since the cause, regardless of the words by which it is expressed, is a grave one, it can be extended to any ecclesiastical impediment from which the Church is accustomed to dispense. This must be admitted since by granting dispensation to those living in concubinage the scandal caused is, to some extent, repaired. Furthermore, a union, even though invalidly formed, often cannot easily be dissolved without causing perhaps greater scandal than the invalid union has already caused. Nor can it be denied that a union thus dissolved would cause injury to the parties involved, especially to the woman and, *a fortiori,* to the children if any have been born of the union.[213]

16. Remarkable Merits. (Excellentia meritorum)

This final cause enumerated by the Propaganda is verified when anyone has rendered great services to religion in combating the enemies of the Catholic Faith, or by his liberality toward the Church, or by his science, his virtue, or in any other way.[214]

This cause, in the fullest sense, is a *causa publica.* It can be

[211] *Cf.* Canon 1094.

[212] *Cf.* Vlaming, *Praelectiones Juris Matrimonii,* II, n. 437.

[213] *Cf.* Payen, *De Matrimonio,* I, n. 750.

[214] S. C. P. F., Instruction, 9 May, 1877, n. 16—*Collect. P. F.,* n. 1470.

invoked by someone who has rendered some outstanding service to the Church or to the Catholic Faith. The person seeking the dispensation may himself be of excellent merits and may be seeking the dispensation for himself or his outstanding merit may be advanced as a cause for obtaining dispensation for others.[215]

The gravity of the cause will depend on the circumstances surrounding the meritorious action used as the basis of the cause. Hence the cause can be grave, more grave or most grave.[216] An action which ordinarily is considered grave can become more grave because of circumstances; for example the petitioner may live in an infidel locality and from his own resources may have built a church.[217] The great good of having built a church becomes in such an instance greater because of the fact that a church in an infidel locality will relatively be of greater good than a church built in a Catholic locality.

The circumstances for verifying this cause could be multiplied indefinitely. The basis of the cause must rest on the excellence of the merits of the one seeking dispensation. Really remarkable merit is required and not the mere giving of alms.[218]

Practical Application

In practice this cause is without value since it can be pleaded only to the Holy See and not the Ordinary.[219]

Too often the charge is made that it is within the power of the wealthy classes to obtain almost any dispensation they desire by making judicious use of donations while those belonging to the poorer classes are too frequently denied dispensation. History bears out the falseness of this charge. At least since the time of Pius V, 1566-1572, dispensation in *forma pauperum* has been in existence in the Church.[220] Through this form dispensation could be obtained by

[215] *Cf.* Vlaming, *Praelectiones Juris Matrimonii,* II, n. 438; Payen, *De Matrimonio,* I, n. 756; Cappello, *De Sacramentis,* III, n. 267.

[216] *Cf.* Cappello, *De Sacramentis,* III, n. 267.

[217] *Cf.* Gasparri, *De Matrimonio,* n. 318, note 4.

[218] *Cf.* De Smet, *Betrothment and Marriage,* II, n. 827, note.

[219] *Cf.* Vlaming, *Praelectiones Juris Matrimonii,* II, n. 438.

[220] *Cf.* Corradus, *Praxis Dispensationum Apostolicarum,* L. VIII, c. 5, n. 4.

those persons who could not afford to pay the usual curial tax imposed for dispensations. That this form for obtaining dispensation could be used only by the poorer classes is evident from the fact that Urban VIII 1623-1644) inserted the word ***miserabiles*** in the petition for dispensation in this form. He did this to counteract the fraud being perpetrated by the nobles of his day who would take a pauper's oath and feign poverty that they might obtain the petitioned dispensation without paying the customary curial tax. The ***forma pauperum***, once instituted in the Church, has never been rescinded and today, no less than in the past, the poorer classes can, through this form, petition and obtain the dispensations which they seek.

CHAPTER VIII

A COMPARISON OF THE CAUSES OF THE PROPAGANDA AND OF THE DATARIA

ARTICLE I. THEIR SIMILARITY

IN the preceding chapter a commentary has been made on the causes enumerated by the Propaganda.[1]

The Apostolic Dataria has also formulated a list containing twenty-eight causes.[2]

An attempt will be made to demonstrate the similarity in the two lists and in a few instances to point out the causes omitted by the Propaganda and proposed by the Apostolic Dataria.

The first three causes proposed by the Dataria for the granting of matrimonial dispensations are listed as follows:

1. Because of smallness of place.
2. Because of smallness of places.
3. Because of the smallness of the place, together with the fact that the dowry of the woman would be insufficient outside the place in question.

In these three causes the Dataria has been specific in stating that a just cause exists for granting matrimonial dispensations when the place in which the petitioner lives, or the places in which the petitioners live, are small or when the town is small, and even though the woman should take residence in a larger town, she will be hampered because of her small dowry.

Through the opinions expressed by any of the authors commenting on the canonical causes it can be seen that the Propaganda comprehended all the above-noted details in the single cause *propter angustiam loci*[3] with perhaps a reference to the second cause proposed by the Propaganda, namely *propter incompetentiam dotis*.

[1] S. C. P. F., Instruction, 9 May, 1877—*Collect. P. F.*, n. 1470.

[2] Ex. S. Dataria Apostolica, *A. S. S.*, XXXIV, pp. 34, 35.

[3] *Cf.* Gasparri, *De Matrimonio*, n. 303, note 1; Vlaming, *Praelectiones Juris Matrimonii*, II, n. 423; Feije, *De Impedimentis*, n. 651.

Furthermore it would seem that there is an intimate connection between the cause *angustia loci* of the Propaganda, and the fifteenth cause enumerated by the Dataria, namely, "because of the difficulty of men in reaching the place for the purpose of contracting marriage with the inhabitants of the locality, *e. g.*, because the place is exposed to the invasion of pirates, or because of the small number of men in the place, *e. g.*, by reason of a war." In the final analysis, the place which is so remotely removed from other places, or which can number only a few men among its inhabitants, is surely a place described by the words *angustia loci*.

The next causes enumerated by the Dataria regard the dowry of the woman, namely:

4. Because of the incompetence of the dowry.

5. Because the small dowry will be increased by the prospective husband.

6. Because the woman is entirely destitute of a dowry.

7. When another will increase the dowry.

With the use of these four causes the Dataria admits the possibility of granting a dispensation when, even though the woman has only a small dowry or is entirely destitute of one, the prospective husband is willing to marry her; or when the prospective husband or someone else is ready to increase the small dowry of the woman. The single cause, *deficientia aut incompetentia dotis* expressed by the Propaganda,[4] implies all the details comprehended by the Apostolic Dataria.[5]

The next three causes of the Dataria regard hatreds arising either from personal animosities or from lawsuits waged in the civil courts. The Dataria has formulated these causes as follows:

10. Because of lawsuits concerning the possession of property.

11. Because of lawsuits involving the dowry.

12. Because of lawsuits involving things of great value.

The Propaganda has provided for any of these three contingencies in the single cause which it formulates in the words: "A lawsuit already begun with regard to an inheritance or the serious or immi-

[4] S. C. P. F., Instruction, 9 May, 1877, n. 3—*Collect. P. F.*, n. 1470.

[5] *Cf.* Vlaming, *Praelectiones Juris Matrimonii,* II, n. 425.

nent danger of such proceedings."[6] The eighth and ninth causes listed by the Dataria are formulated respectively, in the words: "Because of hatreds" and "for the confirmation of peace; and for the sake of bringing about a union between princes and kingdoms." From the words used in its Instruction, it can be seen that the Propaganda extends its single cause, namely, "for the sake of peace" to include both the establishment of peace between rulers and the extinction of hatreds arising among private citizens.

For its thirteenth cause the Dataria mentions that a just cause can be found for dispensing the woman when she is burdened with many children or when she has been bereft of her parents. The canonical cause expressed in the first phrase used by the Dataria, namely, "For the woman burdened with many children," can be likened to the fifth cause proposed by the Propaganda in the phrase, "The poverty of the widow." For a counterpart of the second phrase of the thirteenth cause proposed by the Dataria, namely, "because the woman has been bereft of her parents," it can be recalled that the authors are not adverse to the cause of super-adult age being invoked, for a woman, who, although below the age of twenty-four years, has been bereft of her parents.[7]

The fourteenth cause listed by the Apostolic Dataria and the second cause listed by the Propaganda are identical since they both favor the woman who has attained the age of twenty-four years.[8]

The Apostolic Dataria proposes its sixteenth cause in the words, "For the purpose of placing the Catholic religion of the contractants in safety; and because of the danger of a mixed marriage." By the use of the phrase, "for the purpose of placing the Catholic religion of the contractants in safety," the Apostolic Dataria in its sixteenth cause evidently implies the removal of the danger of apostacy if the dispensation is denied. In its eleventh cause, namely, the danger of a mixed marriage or of a marriage celebrated before an heretical minister, the Propaganda has stated a counterpart to the sixteenth cause of the Dataria.

[6] *Cf.* Chelodi, *Jus Matrimoniale,* n. 46.

[7] *Cf.* Gasparri, *De Matrimonio,* n. 304, note 1; Cappello, *De Sacramentis,* III, n. 261.

[8] *Cf.* S. C. P. F., Instruction, 9 May, 1877, n. 2—*Collect. P. F.,* n. 1470.

The twentieth cause proposed by the Dataria is identical with the sixteenth cause enumerated in the Instruction of the Propaganda. Both agree that excellence of merits in a person can sometimes constitute a canonical cause.

Like the Propaganda, the Dataria also lists so-called *causae inhonestae.* The twenty-second and twenty-third causes, phrased respectively in the words: *"ob infamiam et scandalum"* and *"ob copulam; ob raptum,"* imply and intend to avert or remedy any of the conditions for which the Propaganda was prompted to propose its so-called *causae inhonestae.* Among these disparaging causes of the Propaganda can be numbered: *Nimia, suspecta, periculosa familiaritas, copula, infamia mulieris, remotio gravium scandalorum* and *cessatio publici concubinatus.*[9] It has already been seen that these causes are designed to save the honor of the woman, to assure the welfare of the children and in general to remove or repair scandal.[10]

The twenty-fifth cause proposed by the Dataria, namely, "because of a marriage contracted before a non-Catholic minister," can be likened to the fifteenth cause enumerated by the Propaganda, namely, the "cessation of public concubinage." From the standpoint of the Church when those bound by the form of Catholic marriage contract before a non-Catholic minister the union does not have the appearance of a true marriage and is nothing more than concubinage. The cause as phrased by the Dataria is more specific, that is, a marriage ceremony *in facie ecclesiae* is presupposed to have taken place. Viewed in the light of the cause as expressed by the Propaganda, the concubinage could arise either from a common-law marriage or from a marriage attempted civilly or *coram ministello.*

To continue in the comparison of the causes enumerated by the Dataria and by the Propaganda, it can be noted that, for its twenty-sixth cause the Dataria suggests that a dispensation might be given *"ob matrimonium nulliter contractum."* The Propaganda, on the other hand, phrases its tenth cause in the words *"revalidatio matri-*

[9] *Cf.* S. C. P. F., Instruction, 9 May, 1877, nn. 7, 8, 9, 14, 15—*Collect. P. F.,* n. 1470.

[10] *Cf.* Chelodi, *Jus Matrimoniale,* n. 46; Payen, *De Matrimonio,* I, nn. 748, 755.

monii." It already has been noted that from the exact wording used by the Propaganda this cause as proposed by the Propaganda would apply to a marriage that was invalid because of the presence of some impediment but not to a marriage invalid because of lack of form. This seems certain since in its Instruction the Propaganda uses the words "*revalidatio matrimonii quod, bona fide et publice, servata canonica forma, contractum est.*" The cause as it is phrased by the Dataria will in like manner apply only to a marriage which is invalid because of some impediment. But this cause places no restriction as does the tenth cause of the Propaganda. The Propaganda inserts the words *bona fide* hence noting that fraud on the part of the contractants will render the granting of the dispensation more difficult. The Dataria simply states that a cause for dispensation may be found because the marriage was invalidly contracted.

Article II. Their Dissimilarity

The remainder of the twenty-eight causes enumerated by the Dataria are distinct, from the causes proposed by the Propaganda for they are not mentioned in the Instruction of that congregation. A commentary in so far as is necessary and advisable will be made of these remaining causes proposed by the Apostolic Dataria.

The seventeenth cause of the Dataria reads: "Because of the hope of the conversion of one of the parties to the Catholic religion." To make this cause a more general one it could be formulated simply in the words: "For the cause of conversion." In this way the hope of conversion would not be limited to one of the contractants who happened to be a non-Catholic but it would be extended to include the family of the non-Catholic, or for that matter, several families with which he might be connected. This being the case, the cause of conversion of a whole family would be a public cause or at least a quasi-public cause.[11] The cause is expressed by the Dataria, however, admits the possibility of dispensation when there is a hope of conversion of the non-Catholic party to the mar-

[11] *Cf.* Schenk, *Matrimonial Impediments of Mixed Religion and Disparity of Cult*, n. 296.

riage. If the conversion of the family of the non-Catholic will eventually follow, the cause can all the more readily be admitted in the case of the particular non-Catholic.

While this cause was not mentioned by the Propaganda it is not to be inferred that the idea of it originated with the Dataria. The cause of conversion has apparently been a canonical cause for matrimonial dispensations in the Church since the seventeenth century.[12]

Ordinarily the statement of this cause is so vague that its indiscriminate use can result in many abuses. If it is applied properly, however there are some authors who apparently regard it as a sufficiently just and grave cause.[13] Others admit its use but hold that it should be taken only cumulatively with other causes.[14] To say the least, prudence must be used in making the hope of conversion the foundation for a matrimonial dispensation since oftentimes such a hope of conversion is in reality nothing more than a wish of the Catholic party that the non-Catholic party might convert. Needless to say the hope of conversion must be something beyond a mere wish.

In actual practice it is difficult oftentimes to determine when the cause of conversion may be safely invoked. The moral character of the non-Catholic party will be the first consideration. From this can be determined whether his interest in Catholic belief and practice is real or apparent. If he comes from a family exceptionally known for its bigotry it would seem that he himself would be little inclined to convert after marriage. On the other hand, the influence of the Catholic party over the non-Catholic party should be considered. If the non-Catholic party has already manifested a more than ordinary interest in the Catholic religion, has signified his willingness to take instructions and if, after the marriage the bonds holding the non-Catholic party to his family will be broken so that he

[12] *Cf.* Schenk, *Matrimonial Impediments of Mixed Religion and Disparity of Cult*, n. 297.

[13] *Cf.* Pirhing, *Jus Canonicum*, T. IV, tit. 1, sect. VI, n. 166; Vermeersch, *De Form. Facult. S. C. de Prop. F.*, p. 91.

[14] *Cf.* Wernz, *Jus Decretalium*, IV, n. 586, note 31; Wernz-Vidal, *Jus Canonicum*, V, n. 178, note 30.

will be directly under the influence of his Catholic spouse, it would seem that the cause of conversion could be safely invoked.[15]

For its eighteenth cause the Apostolic Dataria notes "that wealth might be conserved in a family." In short this cause admits the possibility, for instance, of a consanguineous marriage that two wealthy families might be combined or that the family that possesses wealth may not be forced to lose control of it which would be the case if a member of the family should marry outside his own family. While the Dataria admits this cause as being canonical it seems reasonable to agree with Vlaming in holding that it will not stand alone and can be of use only in strengthening the force of other causes admitted in a given case.[16]

The nineteenth cause of the Dataria reads: "For the preservation of an illustrious family, for the preservation of a royal heir." The words used in expressing this cause are sufficiently clear. It quite frequently happens that this cause is invoked so that in practice it is of value. A recent application of this cause was made in the case of Prince Max of Saxony. This nobleman, before he received sacred orders, sought the favor of being permitted to renounce his orders and enter the married state if it should so happen that his brothers should die without issue. He petitioned this favor on the grounds of conserving an illustrious family and Rome permitted him to reserve this right.

In concluding its enumeration of canonical causes the Apostolic Dataria notes in its twenty-seventh cause that a dispensation can be granted "for reasonable causes." In its twenty-eighth cause the Dataria notes further that a dispensation can be granted "for special reasonable causes known to the Holy See." When the first of these causes is invoked the dispensations thus granted are sometimes called dispensations *"sine causa."* In such instances it is not to be inferred that no cause is present but rather that none is specified in the rescript.[17] These two causes differ from each other in that the

[15] *Cf.* Schenk, *Matrimonial Impediments of Mixed Religion and Disparity of Cult,* n. 299.

[16] *Cf.* Vlaming, *Praelectiones Juris Matrimonii,* II, n. 439.

[17] *Cf.* De Smet, *Betrothment and Marriage,* II, n. 828.

circumstances surrounding the twenty-seventh cause are, as it were, honorable, while the circumstances surrounding the twenty-eighth cause are disparaging and should not be published lest, considering the quality of the petitioners, infamy would be brought upon them.[18]

While such causes as these are not found in the Instruction of the Propaganda, the idea of *dispensatio sine causa* is not confined entirely to the Apostolic Dataria. In Canon 1054 it is stated that a dispensation from a minor impediment can be conceded regardless of the presence of obreption or subreption even though the single final cause advanced for the dispensation is false. So far as a minor impediment is concerned, the granting of it when the petition is false is analogous to the granting of a dispensation *sine causa*.

[18] *Cf.* Vlaming, *Praelectiones Juris Matrimonii*, II, n. 438.

APPENDIX A

DISPENSATION IN ROMAN LAW

THE word dispensation is proper to Canon Law. Hence the word is not found in any civil Code nor in any of the texts of the Pandects.[1] Since Roman law antedates Canon law by a long period the doctrine of dispensation never found distinct treatment in any legal treatise. From this fact it is not to be inferred that the Romans did not use dispensations. Through circumlocutions or by the use of various general terms such as privilege, favor of age and so forth it can be seen that in Roman times relaxation of law was not unknown. If the Romans had any idea of the real legal use of the term they never expressed it, for by recalling the canonical significance of the term it can be seen that the Romans divided the use of dispensation between privileges or rescripts according to the cases and the form of its concession.[2] In the Code of Justinian it is found that, although the legislator had made law for the public good, the spirit of Roman law was not adverse to the relaxing of the law in particular cases either through the use of a privilege or through legislation granted in the local courts by rescript, provided, of course, that such actions would be beneficial both to the public good and to the individuals for whom the privilege or rescript was granted.[3]

[1] De Justis, *De Dispensationibus Matrimonialibus*, L. I, c. 1, n. 4.

[2] *Cf.* Cicognani, *Commentarium ad Librum I Codicis*, p. 316.

[3] *Cf.* C. I, 14, 3, *Summa* 3.

APPENDIX B

DISPENSATION IN AMERICAN CIVIL LAW

In American civil law the term dispensation is found and is defined as "the relaxation of a law for the benefit or advantage of an individual." [1] But while the term is found in legal writings the theory of dispensation as such has no place in civil law. In the United States no power exists, except in the legislature, to dispense with law and then it is not so much a dispensation as a change of law. In one particular instance, however, a legal practice exists that is analogous to dispensation from the banns of marriage as found in Canon Law. In about twelve states in the Union advanced notice of marriage must be given. The parties to the contract make application for a marriage license. After an interval of from two to five days they return to the license bureau and only then is the license issued to them.[3] In one state at least, namely Wisconsin, any judge of the court of record may authorize the license to be issued at any time before the time limit has expired, if the parties themselves or the parents or guardians of the woman request it provided it can be proved that either of the parties is in danger of death from illness or that the woman is pregnant.[4]

This suspension of the law of advanced notice of intention to marry is perhaps the only practice in civil law that approaches the canonical use of dispensation in matrimonial cases. But even in this instance it is more akin to the ecclesiastical practice of dispensing from the banns of marriage. In ecclesiastical law it is possible to obtain a dispensation from matrimonial impediments which have been established by ecclesiastical authority. This practice is entirely unknown in American civil procedure.

[1] *Cf. The Cyclopedic Law Dictionary*, Shumacher-Longsdorf, p. 287.

[2] *Cf. Bouvier's Law Dictionary*, p. 583.

[3] *Cf.* Richmond and Hall, *Marriage and the State*, p. 109.

[4] Wisconsin Statutes, 245, 14.

BIBLIOGRAPHY

Sources

Acta Apostolicae Sedis, Romae, Typis Polyglottis Vaticanis, 1909.

Acta Sanctae Sedis, 41 vols., Romae, 1865-1908.

Bullarium Diplomatum et Privilegiorum Sanctorum Romanorum, Editio, 24 vols., Augustae Taurinorum, 1857-1872.

Bullarii Romani Continuatio Summorum Pontificum, 19 vols., Prato, 1756-1883.

Canones et Decreta Sacrosancti Oecumenici Concilii Tridentini, Romae, 1904, et Neapoli, 1859.

Codex Juris Canonici, Pii X Pontificis Maximi jussu digestus Benedicti Papae XV auctoritate promulgatus, Romae, Typis Polyglottis Vaticanis, 1918.

Codicis Juris Canonici Fontes, Cura Emi. Petri Card. Gasparri editi, 6 vols., Romae, 1923-1933.

Collectanea S. Congregationis de Propaganda Fidei, 2 vols., Romae, ex Typographia Polyglotta, 1907.

Corpus Juris Canonici, Editio Lipsiensis II (Richter-Freidberg), 2 vols., Lipsiae, 1922.

Corpus Juris Civilis (Krueger-Mommsen-Schoell-Kroell), 5 ed., 3 vols., Berlin, Weidman, 1928.

Enchiridion Symbolorum Definitionum et Declarationum de rebus Fidei et Morum, Denzinger, Henricus, Friburg, 1932.

Acta Conciliorum et Epistolae Decretales et Constitutiones Summorum Pontificum, Harduinus, Joannes, 12 vols., Parisiis, 1715.

Sacrorum Conciliorum Nova et Amplissima Collectio, Mansi, Joannes, 53 vols., Parisiis, 1901-1927.

Patrologiae Cursus Completus, Migne, J. P., Series Latina, 221 vols., Parisiis, 1844-1845; Series Graeca, 161 vols., Parisiis, 1857-1866.

Monumenta Germaniae Historica, Leges, ed. Gregorius Pertz, 5 vols., Hannoverae, 1875-1889.

Epistolae Romanorum Pontificum Genuinae, Theil, Andreas, Brunsbergae, 1868.

Thesaurus Resolutionum Sacrae Congregationis Concilii, 167 vols., Romae, 1718-1908.

Reference Works

Alzog, John, *Manual of Church History,* 4 vols., ed. nova, Gill and Sons, Dublin, 1879.

Aquinas, St. Thomas, *Opera Omnia,* ed. Frette, Parisiis, 1873-1879.

Ayrinhac-Lydon, *Marriage Legislation in the New Code of Canon Law,* New York, 1932.

Charles Augustine (Bachofen), *A Commentary on the New Code of Canon Law,* 4 ed., 8 vols., St. Louis, Herder, 1921-1929.

Ballerini, Antonius-Palmieri, Dominicus, *Opus Theologicum Morale*, 3 ed., 7 vols., Prati, 1898-1901.

Bangen, Joannes Henricus, *Instructio Practica de Sponsalibus et Matrimonio*, Monasterii, 1858.

Barbosa, Augustinus, *Collectanea Doctorum tam Veterum quam Recentiorum in Jus Pontificium Universum*, Lugduni, 1658.

Benedictus XIV, *De Synodo Dioecesana*, 2 vols., Romae, Typographia S. C. de P. F., 1806.

Bouvier's Law Dictionary, Philadelphia, 1878.

Brys, J., *De Dispensatione in Jure Canonico praesertim apud Decretistas et Decretalistas usque ad Medium Saeculum Decimum Quartum*, Brugis, 1925.

Cappello, Felix, *Tractatus Canonico-Moralis de Sacramentis*, 2 ed., 3 vols., vol. III, *De Matrimonio*, Romae, Marietti, 1933.

Cerato, Prosdocimus, *Matrimonium a Codice Juris Canonici Integre Desumptum*, 4 ed., Padua, Typis Seminar, 1929.

Chelodi, Joannes, *Jus Matrimoniale juxta Codicem Juris Canonici*, 3 ed., Trent, Libr. Edit. Trident., 1921.

———, *Jus de Personis juxta Codicem Juris*, 2 ed., Trent, Libr. Edit. Trident., 1927.

Cicognani, Amletus, I., *Commentarium ad Librum I Codicis*, Romae, 1925.

Cocchi, Guidus, *Commentarium in Codicem Juris Canonici*, 7 vols., Turin, 1925-1927.

Coronata, M. A., *Institutiones Juris Canonici*, vol. I, Turin, 1928.

Corradus, Pyrrhus, *Praxis Dispensationum Apostolicarum pro utroque foro*, ed. in Germania 2a., alias 5a., Coloniae Agrapinae, 1697.

D'Annibale, J., *Summula Theologiae Moralis*, 3 ed., 3 vols., Romae, 1892.

De Becker, Julius, *Praelectiones Canonicae de Matrimonio*, ed. nova, Lovanii, 1931.

De Justis, Vincentius, *De Dispensationibus Matrimonialibus*, Lucae, 1726.

De Marca, Petrus, *De Concordia Sacerdotii et Imperii*, 3 vols., Bambergae, 1788.

De Smet, Aloysius, *Betrothment and Marriage*, 2 vols., St. Louis, 1923-1925.

Durandus, Gulielmus, *Speculum Juris*, 3 vols., Venetiis, 1575.

Farrugia, Nicolaus, *De Matrimonio et Causis Matrimonialibus, Tractatus Canonico-Moralis juxta Codicem Juris Canonici*, Romae, Marietti, 1924.

Feije, Henricus, *De Impedimentis et Dispensationibus Matrimonialibus*, 3 ed., Lovanii, 1885.

Fontanella, Petrus, *De Pactis Nuptialibus*, Genevae, 1659.

Fourneret, Pierre, *Le Mariage Chretien*, Parisiis, Beauchesne, 1925.

Freisen, J., *Geschichte des Canonischen Eherechts*, Paderborn, 1893.

Gasparri, Petrus, *Tractatus Canonicus de Matrimonio*, 3 ed., 2 vols., *Parisiis*, Beauchesne, 1904.

———, *Tractatus Canonicus de Matrimonio*, ed. nova ad mentem Codicis Juris Canonici, Romae, Typis Polyglottis Vaticanis, 1932.

Genicot-Salsmanns, *Institutiones Theologiae Moralis,* 11 ed., 2 vols., Bruxellis, De Wit, 1927.

Giovine, Petrus, *De Dispensationibus Matrimonialibus,* 2 vols., Neapoli, 1863.

Hefele-Leclerque, *Histoire des Conciles,* 5 vols., Parisiis, 1910.

Heiss, M., *Tractatus Quinque de Matrimonio,* Milwaukee, 1861.

Hostiensis (Henricus de Segusio), *Summa Aurea,* Lugduni, 1568.

Lehmkuhl, A., *Theologia Moralis,* 2 vols., Friburgi, 1910.

Ligouri, St. Alphonsus, *Theologia Moralis,* 2 vols., Augustae Taurinorum, 1891.

Lupus, Christianus, *Synodorum Generalium et Provincialium Decreta et Canones,* 12 vols., Venetiis, 1723-1729.

Maroto, Philippus, *Institutiones Juris Canonici,* Romae, 1921.

Michiels, Gommarus, *Normae Generales Juris Canonici,* 2 vols., Lublin, 1929.

Noldin, Henricus, *Summa Theologiae Moralis,* 20 ed., revised by A. Schmitt, 3 vols., Oeniponte, Pustet, 1930.

Ojetti, B., *Commentarium in Codicem Juris Canonici,* 3 vols., Romae, apud Aedes Universitatis Gregorianae, 1928.

O'Keeffe, Gerald M., *Matrimonial Dispensations, Powers of Bishops, Priests and Confessors,* Washington, D. C., Catholic University, 1927.

O'Neill, William H., *Papal Rescripts of Favor,* Washington, D. C., Catholic University, 1930.

Payen, G., *De Matrimonio in Missionibus ac Potissimum in Sinis Tractatus Practicus et Casus,* 3 vols., Zi-ka-wei, in Typographia T'OU-SE-WE, 1928-1929.

Perrone, J., *De Matrimonio Christiano,* 3 vols, Leodii, 1861.

Prümmer, Dominicus, *Manuale Theologiae Moralis,* 4 ed., 3 vols., Freiburg in Breisgau, Herder, 1928.

Putzer, Joseph, *Commentarium in Facultates Apostolicas,* New York, 1897.

Reiffenstuel, Anacletus, *Jus Canonicum Universum,* Parisiis, 1868.

Richmond and Hall, *Marriage and the State,* Russell Sage Foundation, New York, 1929.

Riganti, Joannes, *Commentaria in Regulas Constitutiones et Ordinationes Cancellariae Apostolicae,* 4 vols. in 2, Coloniae Allobrogum, 1751.

Roskavany, Augustinus, *Matrimonium in Ecclesia Catholica,* 4 vols., Pestini, 1870.

Sanchez, Thomas, S.J., *De Sancto Matrimonii Sacramento Disputationum Tomi Tres,* 3 vols., Lugduni, 1669.

Sanctus, Bernardus, *Opera Omnia,* Mediolano, 1850.

Schenk, Francis, *The Matrimonial Impediments of Mixed Religion and Disparity of Cult,* Washington, D. C., Catholic University, 1929.

Schmalzgrueber, Franciscus, *Jus Ecclesiasticum Universum,* 12 vols., Romae, 1844.

Singer, H., *Die Summa Decretorum des Magister Rufinus,* Panderborn, 1902.

Sipos, Stephanus, *Enchiridion Juris Canonici,* Pecs, 1926.

Soglia, Joannes Cardinalis, *Institutiones Juris Privati Ecclesiastici,* 2 vols., Parisiis, 1842.

Stiegler, M. A., *Dispensation, Dispensationswesen und Dispensationsrecht im Kirchenrecht geschichtlich dargestellt,* Mainz, 1901.

Ter Haar, Francis, C.SS.R.-Connell, Francis J., C.SS.R., *Mixed Marriages and Their Remedies,* New York, 1933.

Thomassinus, Ludovicus, *Vetus et Nova Ecclesiae Disciplina,* 10 vols., Magentiaci, 1786-1787.

Van Espen, Bernardus, *Jus Ecclesiasticum Universum,* 5 vols., Lovanii, 1753.

Vecchiotti, Septimii, *Institutiones Canonicae,* 3 vols., Marietti, Romae, 1886.

Vermeersch-Creusen, *Epitome Juris Canonici,* 5 ed., 3 vols., Mechliniae-Romae, Dessain, 1933.

Vlaming, Thomas M., *Praelectiones Juris Matrimonii,* 3 ed., 2 vols., Bussum in Hollandia, 1919.

Wahl, Francis X., *The Matrimonial Impediments of Consanguinity and Affinity,* Washington, D. C., Catholic University, 1934.

Wernz, Franciscus, *Jus Decretalium,* vol. IV in 2, Prati, ex Off. Lib. Giochetti, 1911-1913.

Wernz-Vidal, *Jus Matrimoniale,* 2 ed., Romae, apud Aedes Universitatis Gregorianae, 1928.

Zitelli, Z., *Apparatus Juris Ecclesiastici,* 3 ed., Ratisbonae, 1903.

UNIVERSITAS CATHOLICA AMERICAE

WASHINGTON, D. C.

FACULTAS JURIS CANONICI

No. 96

1935

ALPHABETICAL INDEX

VITA

William A. O'Mara was born in Butte, Mont., September 15, 1905, and attended St. Joseph's Parochial School in that city. In 1927 he obtained the degree of Bachelor of Arts from St. Thomas College, Scranton, Pa. His theological course was made in St. Bonaventure's Seminary, Allegany, N. Y., and he was ordained to the priesthood May 30, 1931. In September, 1932, he entered the Catholic University, Washington, D. C., to pursue a course of graduate studies in the School of Canon Law.

CANON LAW STUDIES

1. Freriks, Rev. Celestine A., C.PP.S., J.C.D., Religious Congregations in Their External Relations, 121 pp., 1916.
2. Gallther, Rev. Daniel M., O.P., J.C.D., Canonical Elections, 117 pp., 1917.
3. Borkowski, Rev. Aurelius L., O.F.M. De Confraternitatibus Ecclesiasticis, 136 pp., 1918.
4. Castillo, Rev. Cayo, J.C.D., Disertacion Historico-canonica sobre la Potestad del Cabildo en Sede Vacante o Impedida del Vicario Capitular, 99 pp., 1919 (1918).
5. Kubelbeck, Rev. William J., S.T.B., J.C.D., The Sacred Penitentiaria and Its Relations to Faculties of Ordinaries and Priests, 129 pp., 1918.
6. Petrovits, Rev. Joseph, J. C., S.T.D., J.C.D., The New Church Law on Matrimony, X-461 pp., 1919.
7. Hickey, Rev. John J., S.T.B., J.C.D., Irregularities and Simple Impediments in the New Code of Canon Law, 100 pp., 1920.
8. Klekotka, Rev. Peter J., S.T.B., J.C.D., Diocesan Consultors, 179 pp., 1920.
9. Wannenmacher, Rev. Francis, J.C.D., The Evidence in Ecclesiastical Procedure Affecting the Marriage Bond, 1920. (Not Printed.)
10. Golden, Rev. Henry Francis, J.C.D., Parochial Benefices in the New Code, IV-119 pp., (Printed 1925.)
11. Koudelka, Rev. Charles, J., J.C.D., Pastors, Their Rights and Duties According to the New Code of Canon Law, 211 pp., 1921.
12. Melo, Rev. Antonius, O.F.M., J.C.D., De Exemptione Regularium, X-188 pp., 1921.
13. Schaaf, Rev. Valentine Theodore, O.F.M., S.T.D., J.C.D., The Cloister X-180 pp., 1921.
14. Burke, Rev. Thomas Joseph, S.T.B., J.C.D., Competence in Ecclesiastical Tribunals, IV-117 pp., 1922.
15. Leech, Rev. George Leo, J.C.D., A Comparative Study of the Constitution "Apostolicae Sedis" and the "Codex Juris Canonici," 179 pp., 1922.
16. Motry, Rev. Hubert Louis, S.T.D., J.C.D., Diocesan Faculties According to the Code of Canon Law, II-167 pp., 1922.
17. Murphy, Rev. George Lawrence, J.C.D., Delinquencies and Penalties in the Administration and the Reception of the Sacraments, IV-121 pp., 1923.
18. O'Reilly, Rev. John Anthony, S.T.B., J.C.D., Ecclesiastical Sepultuae in the New Code of Canon Law, II-129 pp., 1923.
19. Michalicka, Rev. Wenceslas Cyrill, O.S.B., J.C.D., Judicial Procedure in Dismissal of Clerical Exempt Religious, 107 pp., 1923.

20. Dargin, Rev. Edward Vincent, S.T.B., J.C.D., Reserved Cases According to the Code of Canon Law, IV-103 pp., 1924.
21. Godfrey, Rev. John A., S.T.B., J.C.D., The Right of Patronage According to the Code of Canon Law, 153 pp., 1924.
22. Hagedorn, Rev. Francis Edward, J.C.D., General Legislation on Indulgences, II-154 pp., 1924.
23. King, Rev. James Ignatius, J.C.D., The Administration of the Sacraments to Dying Non-Catholics, V-141 pp., 1924.
24. Winslow, Rev. Francis Joseph, A.F.M., J.C.D., Vicars and Prefects Apostolic, IV-149 pp., 1924.
25. Correa, Rev. Jose Servelion, S.T.L., J.C.D., La Potestad Legislativa de la Iglesia Católica, IV-127 pp., 1925.
26. Dugan, Rev. Henry Francis, M.A., J.C.D., The Judiciary Department of the Diocesan Curia, 87 pp., 1925.
27. Keller, Rev. Charles Frederick, S.T.D., J.C.D., Mass Stipends, 167 pp., 1925.
28. Paschang, Rev. John Linus, J.C.D., The Sacramentals According to the Code of Canon Law, 129 pp., 1925.
29. Piontek, Rev. Cyrillus, O.F.M., S.T.B., J.C.D., De Indulto Exclaustrationis necnon Saecularizationis, XIII-289 pp., 1925.
30. Kearney, Rev. Richard Joseph, S.T.B., J.C.D., Sponsors at Baptism According to the Code of Canon Law, IV-127 pp., 1925.
31. Bartlett, Rev. Chester Joseph, A.M., LL.B., J.C.D., The Tenure of Parochial Property in the United States of America, V-108 pp., 1926.
32. Kilker, Rev. Adrian Jerome, J.C.D., Extreme Unction, V-425 pp., 1926
33. McCormick, Rev. Robert Emmett, J.C.D., Confessors of Religious, VIII-266 pp., 1926.
34. Miller, Rev. Newton Thomas, J.C.D., Founded Masses According to the Code of Canon Law, VII-93 pp., 1926.
35. Roelker, Rev. Edward G., S.T.D., J.C.D., Principles of Privilege According to the Code of Canon Law, XI-166 pp., 1926.
36. Bakalarczyk, Rev. Richardus, M.I.C., J.U.D., De Novitiatu, VIII-208 pp., 1927.
37. Pizzuti, Rev. Lawrence, O.F.M., J.U.L., De Parochis Religiosis, 1927. (Not Printed.)
38. Bliley, Rev. Nicholas Martin, O.S.B., J.C.D., Altars According to the Code of Canon Law, XIX-132 pp., 1927.
39. Brown, Brendan Francis, A.B., LL.M., J.U.D., The Canonical Juristic Personality with Special Reference to its Status in the United States of America, V-212 pp., 1927.
40. Cavanaugh, Rev. William Thomas, C.P., J.U.D., The Reservation of the Blessed Sacrament, VIII-101 pp., 1927.
41. Doheny, Rev. William J., C.S.C., A.B., J.U.D., Church Property: Modes of Acquisition, X-118, pp., 1927.

42. Feldhaus, Rev. Aloysius H., C.PP.S., J.C.D., Oratories, IX-141 pp., 1927.
43. Kelly, Rev. James Patrick, A.B., J.C.D., The Jurisdiction of the Simple Confessor, X-208 pp., 1927.
44. Neuberger, Rev. Nicholas J., J.C.D., Canon 6 or the Relation of the Codex Juris Canonici to the Preceding Legislation, V-95 pp., 1927.
45. O'Keeffe, Rev. Gerald Michael, J.C.D., Matrimonial Dispensations, Powers of Bishops, Priests, and Confessors, VIII-232 pp., 1927.
46. Quigley, Rev. Joseph, A.M., A.B., J.C.D., Condemned Societies, 139 pp., 1927.
47. Zaplotnik, Rev. Ioannes Leo, J.C.D., De Vicariis Foraneis, X-142 pp., 1927.
48. Duskie, Rev. John Aloysius, A.B., J.C.D., The Canonical Status of the Orientals in the United States, VIII-196 pp., 1928.
49. Hyland, Rev. Francis Edward, J.C.D., Excommunication, Its Nature, Historical Development and Effects, VIII-181 pp., 1928.
50. Reinmann, Rev. Gerald Joseph, O.M.C., J.C.D., The Third Order Secular of Saint Francis, 201 pp., 1928.
51. Schenk, Rev. Francis J., J.C.D., The Matrimonial Impediments of Mixed Religion and Disparity of Cult, XVI-318 pp., 1929.
52. Coady, Rev. John Joseph, S.T.D., J.U.D., A.M., The Appointment of Pastors, VIII-150 pp., 1929.
53. Kay, Rev. Thomas Henry, J.C.D., Competence in Matrimonial Procedure, VIII-164 pp., 1929.
54. Turner, Rev. Sidney Joseph, C.P., J.U.D., The Vow of Poverty, XLIX-217 pp., 1929.
55. Kearney, Rev. Raymond A., A.B., S.T.D., J.C.D., The Principles of Delegation, VII-149 pp., 1929.
56. Conran, Rev. Edward James, A.B., J.C.D., The Interdict, V-163 pp., 1930.
57. O'Neil, Rev. William H., J.C.D., Papal Rescripts of Favor, VII-218 pp., 1930.
58. Bastnagel, Rev. Clement Vincent, J.U.D., The Appointment of Parochial Adjutants and Assistants, XV-257 pp., 1930.
59. Ferry, Rev. William A., A.B., J.C.D., Stole Fees, X-107 pp., 1930.
60. Costello, Rev. John Michael, A.B., J.C.D., Domicile and Quasi-Domicile, VII-201 pp., 1930.
61. Kremer, Rev. Michael Nicholas, A.B., S.T.B., J.C.D., Church Support in the United States, VI-136 pp., 1930.
62. Angulo, Rev. Luis, C.M., J.C.D., Legislación de la Iglesia sobre la intención en la applicación de la Santa Misa, VII-104 pp., 1931.
63. Frey, Rev. Wolfgang Norbert, O.S.B., A.B., J.C.D., The Act of Religious Profession, VIII-174 pp., 1931.
64. Roberts, Rev. James Brendan, A.B., J.C.D., The Banns of Marriage, XIV-140 pp., 1931.
65. Ryder, Rev. Raymond Aloysius, A.B., J.C.D., Simony, IX-151 pp., 1931.

66. Campagna, Rev. Angelo, Ph.D., J.U.D., Il Vicario Generale del Vescovo, VII-205 pp., 1931.
67. Cox, Rev. Joseph Godfrey, A.B., J.C.D., The Administration of Seminaries, VI-124 pp., 1931.
68. Gregory, Rev. Donald J., J.U.D., The Pauline Privilege, XV-165 pp., 1931.
60. Donohue, Rev. John F., J.C.D., The Impediment of Crime, VIII-110 pp., 1931.
70. Dooley, Rev. Eugene A., O.M.I., J.C.D., Church Law on Sacred Relics, IX-143 pp., 1931.
71. Orth, Rev. Clement Raymond, O.M.C., J.C.D., The Approbation of Religious Institutes, 171 pp., 1931.
72. Pernicone, Rev. Joseph M., A.B., J.C.D., The Ecclesiastical Prohibition of Books, XII-267 pp., 1932.
73. Clinton, Rev. Connell, A.B., J.C.D., The Paschal Precept, IX-108 pp., 1932.
74. Donnelly, Rev. Francis B., A.M., S.T.L., J.C.D., The Diocesan Synod, VIII-125 pp., 1932.
75. Torrente, Rev. Camilo, C.M.F., J.C.D., Las Processiones Sagradas, V-145 pp., 1932.
76. Murphy, Rev. Edwin J., C.PP.S., J.C.D., Suspension Ex Informata Conscientia, XI-122 pp., 1932.
77. MacKenzie, Rev. Eric F., A.M., S.T.L., J.C.D., The Delict of Heresy in its Commission, Penalization, Absolution, VII-124 pp., 1932.
78. Lyons, Rev. Avitus E., S.T.B., J.C.D., The Collegiate Tribunal of First Instance, XI-147 pp., 1932.
79. Connolly, Rev. Thomas A., J.C.D., Appeals, XI-195 pp., 1932.
80. Sangmeister, Rev. Joseph V., A.B., J.C.D., Force and Fear as Precluding Matrimonial Consent, V-211 pp., 1932.
81. Jaeger, Rev. Leo A., A.B., J.C.D., The Administration of Vacant and Quasi-Vacant Episcopal Sees in the United States, IX-229 pp., 1932.
82. Rimlinger, Rev. Herbert T., J.C.D., Error Invalidating Matrimonial Consent, VII-79 pp., 1932.
83. Barrett, Rev. John D. M., S.S., J.C.D., Comparative Study of the Third Plenary Council and the Code, IX-221 pp., 1932.
84. Carberry, Rev. John J., Ph.D., S.T.D., J.C.L., The Juridical Form of Marriage, X-177 pp., 1934.
85. Dolan, Rev. John L., A.B., J.C.L., The Defensor Vinculi, XII-157 pp., 1934.
86. Hannan, Rev. Jerome D., A.M., S.T.D., LL.B., J.C.L., The Cannon Law of Wills, IX-517 pp., 1934.
87. Lemieux, Rev. Lelisle A., A.M., J.C.L., The Sentence in Ecclesiastical Proceduce, IX-131 pp., 1934.
88. O'Rourke, Rev. James J., A.B., J.C.L., Parish Registers, VII-109 pp., 1934.

89. Timlin, Rev. Bartholomew, O.F.M., A.M., J.C.L., Conditional Matrimonial Consent, X-381 pp., 1934.
90. Wahl, Rev. Francis X., A.B., J.C.L., The Matrimonial Impediments of Consanguinity and Affinity, VI-125 pp., 1934.
91. White, Rev. Robert J., A.B., LL.B., S.T.B., J.C.L., Canonical Ante-Nuptial Promise and the Civil Law, VI-152 pp., 1934.
92. Herrera, Rev. Anthony Parra, O.C.D., J.C.L., Legislacion Ecclesiastica sobre el Ayuno y la Abstinencia, 1935.
93. Reilly, Rev. Peter, J.C.L., Residence of Pastors, 1935.
Cases of Evident Nullity, 1935.
94. Manning, Rev. John J., A.B., J.C.L., Presumption of Law in Matrimonial Procedure, 1935.
95. Moeder, Rev. John M., J.C.L., The Proper Bishop for Ordination and Dismissorial Letters, 1935.
96. O'Mara, Rev. William A., Canonical Causes for Matrimonial Dispensations, 1935.
97. Reilly, Rev. Peter, J.C.L., Residence of Pastors, 1935.
98. Smith, Rev. Mariner T., O.P., S.T.Lr., J.C.L., The Penal Law for Religious, 1935.
99. Whalen, Rev. Donald W., A.M., J.C.L., The Value of Testimonial Evidence in Matrimonial Procedure, 1935.

www.ingramcontent.com/pod-product-compliance
Lightning Source LLC
LaVergne TN
LVHW050225080826
844660LV00012B/468

* 9 7 8 0 8 1 3 2 2 2 8 5 1 *